# LED BY A LION

## Principles for Leadership And Their Biblical Roots

Christopher Cone, ThD, PhD, PhD

Exegetica Publishing
2023

"I am not afraid of an army of lions led by a sheep; I am afraid of an army of sheep led by a lion."

– Alexander the Great

*Led By a Lion: Principles for Leadership and Their Biblical Roots*

©2023 Christopher Cone, ThD, PhD, PhD

Published by Exegetica Publishing
Fort Dodge, Iowa

ISBN: 978-1-60265-094-7

All Scripture quotations, except those noted otherwise are from the New American Standard Bible, ©1960, 1962, 1963, 1968, 1971, 1972, 1973, 1975, 1977, and 1995 by the Lockman Foundation.

# TABLE OF CONTENTS

# PREFACE

The most effective leadership, management, and efficiency models share traits common with each other, and traits that are ultimately traceable to the pages of the Bible. While these models are often not intentionally rooted in Biblical concepts by those that promote the models, the models illustrate how applying Biblical principles can set a trajectory of success in enterprise and in life. *Led By a Lion* is designed to introduce some of these leadership, management, and efficiency models, but goes a step further in identifying the Biblical genesis of many of the core traits that fuel the success of these models.

Just as the Bible is not a science textbook or a history textbook, it is also not a leadership textbook – its message is not centered on these three aspects. There is another thematic priority, for sure. However, just as the Bible provides a launching pad for accurately understanding science and history, it also offers tremendous grounding for effective leadership, skillful management, quality organizational oversight, efficient goal-oriented processes, and understanding the true meaning of success.

Ultimately, as the reader becomes familiar with the brilliance and elegance of Biblical methodologies in these areas, perhaps the reader will consider how valuable God's prescriptions are for other areas of life as well. Indeed, we have much to learn from the greatest Leader humanity has ever seen: the Lion of Judah...

# BASICS
# AND
# PRIORITIES

# 1
# FOUNDATIONS
# OF LEADERSHIP

To *lead* is from an old English word (*loeden*) meaning to travel or to guide. Dwight Eisenhower once described leadership as "the art of getting someone else to do something you want done because he wants to do it." Tom Landry suggested leadership means "getting someone to do what they don't want to do in order to achieve what they want to achieve." A person has a goal and perhaps even understands where to go, but they're not quite sure how to get there. As a leader your job is to help them get there.

The idea of leadership appears early in the Bible in Exodus 13:21 and the Hebrew word that is used in this verse means *to guide or to lead*. We read that the Lord (Yahweh in Hebrew) is going before Israel in a pillar of cloud by day to lead them on the way and a pillar of fire by night to give them light that they might travel by day and by night. God Himself is leading the people by going before them and showing them the path. He provides a helpful illustration of leadership and underscores the great responsibility that leaders have.

There are three basic perspectives for foundations of leadership: (1) naturalistic humanistic, (2) supernatural/evil, and (3) super-natural/righteous. In the naturalistic humanistic perspective, there is nothing beyond the natural realm. Frederick Nietzsche describes in this approach a herd mentality tying the leadership dynamic to human impulses and activities. The basic manner of life shows valuations and orders of rank as expressions of the need of a community or herd. A community (or herd) needs moral direction, and the individual is taught to become part of the function of the herd. Morality is not something that is divinely given, but rather is from the herd's establishing traditions and the behaviors necessary for the well-being of the herd. Nietzsche describes that the conditions for the maintenance of one community may differ from those of another and necessitates different kinds of leadership. Ultimately Nietzsche condemns the herd morality, preferring that individuals exercise the *will to power*. A person should be able to get out of that herd mentality and lead instead. For Nietzsche it is about the herd – either being a part of the herd or simply leading the herd – for the herd's survival. Nietzsche's model is a social Darwinian, evolutionary kind.

If on the other hand we take a Biblical perspective, we can discern two directions in which beyond-the-natural or supernatural aspects are evident. In the supernatural/evil leadership model we encounter this incredibly magnificent leader called Satan. Jesus has some interesting things to say about this one. In John 8, for example Jesus is critiquing people who are very arrogant and causing destruction for others. Jesus tells them that "you are of your father the devil and you want to do the desires of your father. He was a murderer from the beginning and does not stand in the truth because there is no truth in him. Whenever he speaks a lie he speaks from his own nature for he is a liar and the father of lies."[1] According to Jesus this great leader, Satan, is the father of lies. On the one hand Nietzsche is telling us we have an entire structure of community and leadership that originates through community, that it is just based on the needs of the herd; ultimately that this is really all meaningless and so we must make our own value. On

---

[1] John 8:44.

the other hand, we have the devil, called the father of lies, whose leadership we can't trust. Recall Genesis 3 when Satan came to Eve and showed her a different path to arrive at the destination that God had already promised her. That alternate path promised she would be like God, but instead of it resulting in her being like God, it resulted in death, destruction, and condemnation. In Ephesians 2:2 we are told that that he has armies and forces – he is not working alone. Instead, there are armies and hierarchies and organizations and structures that he is leading. Satan is a very adept leader and in fact his leadership has been well recognized. In Alinsky's *Rules for Radicals*, for example, Alinsky's instructs would-be radicals on the recipe and tools to change culture and society. In the intro to the book Alinsky acknowledges Lucifer (another of Satan's names) as the original radical who gained his own kingdom.[2] Satan is the very first radical known to man – one who comes in and changes culture and society through rebellion against the establishment. Who is the *establishment* in that context? God the Creator. Satan's rebellion and leadership was so effective that (as Alinsky notes) Satan at least won his own kingdom.

The snapshot of Genesis 1-3 shows that Satan was initially very successful. It seems that Satan absolutely earned his own kingdom and destroyed everything that God had set in place. In fact, after God created, God declared it all to be very good. Yet just a few chapters later in the historical account we discover that God was grieved because man was so evil. In a sense, Alinsky was right. However, Satan's success was short-lived. If we read the rest of the story, we see that Satan and his evil kingdom is ultimately conquered by good.

---

[2] Saul Alinsky, *Rules for Radicals: A Practical Primer for Realistic Radicals* (Vintage, 1989), ix.

It is certainly worth questioning the value of an effective leader if the destination that people are being led is their own destruction. That is not good leadership at all. Effective? Certainly – because many followed. Good? Most certainly not. Satan's model of leadership is deceptive and destructive – and ultimately the foundation of Nietzsche's naturalistic approach – both provide an alternative to God's leadership model.

The third option is the supernatural/righteous model. In Biblical cosmology God's plan is revealed for the expression of His character (or glory). He uses different colors in this tapestry, and evil is one of those colors. While evil has a temporary role in this cosmology, ultimately God wins. The Creator who is sovereign over all, finishes the tapestry, if you will, through His own chosen Leader.

Isaiah 11 introduces us to this Leader as a shoot springing from the stem of Jesse. The Leader will be a human being – a branch from the line of Jesse – and the spirit of the Lord will rest on Him; also, the spirit of wisdom, understanding, counsel, strength, and knowledge and the fear of the Lord; He will delight in the fear of the Lord; He will not judge by what His eyes see or by what His ears hear, but with righteousness will judge the poor and decide with fairness for the afflicted of the earth. He will strike the earth with the rod of His mouth and a breath of His lips will slay the wicked. Righteousness will be the belt about his loins, faithfulness the belt about his waist.

These are all so relevant to good leadership, and any leader would want these qualities. Consider Philippians 2, for example. There we find Paul exhorting his readers to have the kind of thinking in themselves which is also in Christ Jesus. He existed as God, yet didn't regard equality with God a thing to be held onto or maintained. Instead, He emptied himself, leaving behind His glory. He took on the form of a bondservant. Being made in the likeness of men, He went to the cross to die for the benefit of others. This is where Jesus's leadership obliterates Nietzsche's system, which says that because you can't know anything for certain, you can only preserve yourself. Jesus is saying (and showing) just the opposite – we should be willing to give ourselves up for others. What Jesus values is the very opposite of what Nietzsche values – these two represent totally conflicting models of leadership.

Nietzsche goes so far as to suggest that Christianity is the greatest evil perpetuated on humanity because Jesus promoted self-sacrifice.[3] Jesus tells His own followers that if anyone wishes to serve Him, that person must follow Jesus, and that His Father will honor that person. Jesus suggests that those who will follow His leadership have to also do what He does, and the Father will honor that person for following Jesus. Jesus's leadership model is very different than the other two. In a leadership context, we can choose a humanistic, naturalistic approach or we can look at a supernatural approach with two competing models (evil vs. righteous). Because of Jesus's example, we will ultimately choose the supernatural/righteous approach that is advocated in Biblical cosmology.

As we look through that Biblical lens at the leadership landscape, we discover a diversity of tools with beneficial elements. Let's explore some common leadership models and consider how they look through the Biblical lens. One leadership institute identifies four styles of leadership: the visionary, the achiever, the facilitator, and the

---

[3] E.g., "What is more harmful than any vice?...Christianity." Friedrich Nietzsche, *Antichrist* (Global Grey Ebooks, 2018), 18. "Nothing is more unhealthy...than Christian pity." Ibid., 21. "The Christian concept of God is...one of the most corrupt concepts that has ever been set up in the world" Ibid., 29.

analyzer.[4] The **visionary** is able to look ahead and identify where things need to go and is able to inspire a team to be able to get there. The potential downside of the visionary is perhaps they don't quite know how to get there, and perhaps they don't lead the team well or are not patient enough with people on the journey. The **achiever** has high capacity and can lead by example and get things done. The potential downside of the achiever is that person can have such high expectations that the team may not be able to meet them. The **facilitator** (which some might call the coach) is the one who is making it all happen. They are involved in helping and may potentially be too involved in the details. For the facilitator it may become a bit more difficult to see and achieve the big picture vision because of the individual attention necessary to mentor or coach well. The **analyzer** is the one who can diagnose and prescribe change. They will help keep the team out of trouble. They might not be well equipped for the visionary aspect, and thus not particularly inspiring. Also, they might be somewhat critical and potentially discouraging to those around them. Each of these leadership styles have great advantages, but they also have limitations. If you favor one of these four leadership styles and you ignore the other three, you will probably find it difficult to lead well. A point of application is worthwhile here: we need to maximize our own personal tools in these areas, but we also need to surround ourselves with others who have skill in aspects of leadership in areas we might be less capable.

These four styles provide a good point of entry for our discussion, as they illustrate advantages and disadvantages of common

---

[4] Dale Carnegie Training Center, "Define Your Leadership Style and Tendencies," April 10, 2012, viewed at https://dalecarnegiewaynj.com/2012/04/10/define-your-leadership-style-and-tendencies/.

leadership approaches. There are other styles to consider. The **democratic** leadership style allows everybody to have a voice and can be very effective because of how it involves and empowers others. Of course, one major challenge presented by this style is that the more voices there are, the slower things will probably move, and the more difficult progress can be. Still, this approach can keep things more balanced and keep more people engaged.

The **autocratic** leader sometimes can be very effective as the monarch who directs the organization. However, the autocratic approach can squelch other voices, limiting the creativity and effectiveness of others. Because of these significant limitations, the autocratic approach is not generally the most effective.

**Laizzes-faire** is a hands-off approach. It is the leadership equivalent to deism (the view in which God created and then lets the creation run on its own). This hands-off model puts things in place for those being led to handle things themselves, with leadership being delegated broadly. At some level, those who are bearing the burden of leadership are empowered but will have to choose a leadership model. They can't all operate using the laissez-faire approach. At some level or another, active leadership is needed.

**Strategic leadership** is generally more focused on the goals and objectives and can be very effective. However, if the focus at the leadership level shifts to the details, processes rather than outcomes can garner too much attention for the leaders to be effective.

**Servant leadership** pours into people, invests in people, and serves people – there is no downside to leading with these as priorities. Servant leadership requires commitment and patience and can be very effective. When a leader is willing to give of themselves to help someone else achieve the goal, that resonates with those who are following.

**Transactional leadership** is a leadership style that helps people move forward by engaging with one another not in a personal way but through a barter system of exchange and *quid pro quo*. In this approach the more transactions there are, the more is accomplished. Transactional leadership does little to invest in people, as mission fulfillment is more reliant on completion of tasks. It is not uncommon for leaders to intend to use a democratic, strategic, or even servant approach, yet in practice the value created for employees is simply in the dollars being compensated. That is transactional leadership – initially very effective but limiting in its capacity to help people reach their potential.

**Coaching leadership** focuses on helping people develop so that they can achieve goals. If a leader can help a person on their team accomplish what that person needs to accomplish or to be what they need to be in this task, then the team will be better for it. The team will be closer to meeting its goals. If the coaching leader can do that with each person on the team, then the team can achieve excellence. The downside of that is while the leader's attention is focused on one person, another is needing guidance and direction. To meet the multiplying need requires a coaching staff and not just one person coaching. If a leader can't develop other leaders and delegate effectively, the coaching leadership style will lead to ineffectiveness, bottlenecks, and resulting frustrations.

Each of the models introduced above has advantages and disadvantages. **Transformative leadership** attempts to draw on the advantages of each while minimizing the negatives. Transformative leadership is rooted in transformative learning (the idea that effective learning should result in transformation), is intent on the transformation of those being led, and employs diverse leadership approaches (borrowing from each of the above) at times to help facilitate personal transformation. Biblical wisdom asserts that real transformation comes by the renewing of the mind,[5] thus the goal of transformative leadership is to help lead people through that process. In the transformative model people aren't simply resources to fulfill the organizational mission. Leaders are not simply providing people with a voice (as in a democratic model), not simply trying to make sure they are following well (as in the autocratic model), not simply empowering them (as in a laissez-faire model), not simply ensuring effective strategies and tools (as in the strategic model) – and so on. Instead, the goal of leadership is to do what can be done to ensure the personal growth of those who are being led. As they grow they become much more effective in helping the organization achieve its mission.

Still, that organizational element is secondary. Organizations are never more valuable than people (people are created in God's image, companies are not). An organization that is focused on the growth of people should reflect that commitment in its mission – thus there ought to be no conflict between the priorities of organizational mission fulfillment and personal transformation. The *byproduct* of this kind of leadership is that when people grow, they are best able to accomplish what they are designed for. If they are growing in this way, and if they do their part, then the organization has something much greater than simply a person who can fill a job.

---

[5] Romans 12:1-2 contrasts the kind of thinking that is in accordance with what God has designed and communicated and the kind of thinking that is according to a broken world system and culture. If God is the designer, then applying His (Biblical) lens to various disciplines and vocations – and every area of life – results in people being their best and ultimately their most effective.

The ongoing challenge for one who desires to be a transformative leader is found in balancing the duty to the organization and the responsibility to the individual. In this kind of transformative leadership, the individual comes first, and organizational success is the result, and not the other way around. Transformative leadership is committed to helping people grow and to providing them the avenues to express that growth in service through the use of the tools that God has given them. As they commit to their own development, their contribution to the team also develops. Of course, this can happen with different kinds of leaders employing various leadership styles, but a transformative leadership style is committed to the growth of people as individuals, understanding that mature individuals are simply better team members. The transformative leadership model is incredibly effective.

Let's examine some of the aspects of transformative leadership. First of all we can say that it's situational. If we go back and look at all these different models that we talked about – in a democratic model, if you slip into autocratic you've destroyed your system. You will lose your people because you've set a culture. If you're in an autocratic model and you do the laissez faire model you've destroyed your culture. In other words – you have to stick with your model and you don't really vary. All of them are going to be somewhat situational but in a transformative model it's situational in this sense. You need to know the context—what you are dealing with—and you need to know your people. If you know your people and your first priority is to love these people—to care for them, invest in them, and help them be who they can be—then they will do what they're designed to do, but in order to lead in that context you have to understand what *is* the context that they're in and who these people are.

Because people are different, they respond to different models of leadership. They respond to different stimuli. They have different motivations. They are in different contexts. For example, someone who has a great deal of financial pressure in their life but has all the tools is going to respond differently and need a different kind of leadership than someone who has no financial pressure and has all the same tools. There are different dynamics, so it is situational.

Next, think about Maslow's hierarchy versus a transformative hierarchy. At the top of Maslow's hierarchy we start with the physiological needs. According to Abraham Maslow we pursue these things constantly – food, drink, sex, warmth/cold (depending on where we are). And then we pursue safety. According to Maslow we value these physiological needs more than safety and then love and belonging – being a part of a community and esteem. Are we respected within that community? And then we value self-actualization – fulfillment. That's the top of the pyramid which fits perfectly with Nietzsche's naturalistic leadership dynamic. The problem is if you trace that out and you are consistent with it, it really is meaningless. But what is self-actualization? What does that even mean? When have you arrived at it? Who defines it? These are basic worldview questions that most aspiring to leadership aren't really thinking about, yet I suggest that if you are not concerned about the people you're leading – to the very core of their existence, understanding who they are, what they are about, what they need – then you're really not going to be a long term benefit to them except for opening some doors and giving them some experience. You can be so much more than that.

So, let's flip it. This is what I would refer to as the transformative hierarchy. Just completely flip it upside down. What is the first priority? Divine relationship. Humanity is designed to have a relationship with humanity's creator. We see that in John 17:3. Jesus actually says eternal life is to know God. Everybody wants to live forever. Everybody wants to go to heaven. The whole point of all that is to have this intimate knowledge of the Divine Person. That's the number one priority. I think if we're doing this right that is far more important to us than food and water and any other elements of life. When we read some of the Psalms, for example, we see how David is a great leader. He made all kinds of mistakes, but he's still a great leader. We read how this model of leadership desires this kind of intimacy with his Creator above all else. David teaches his son, and then we read in Proverbs, David's son (Solomon) teaches his own son. This underscores how knowing God is the point. That's really at the core of all of us – this need for divine relationship.

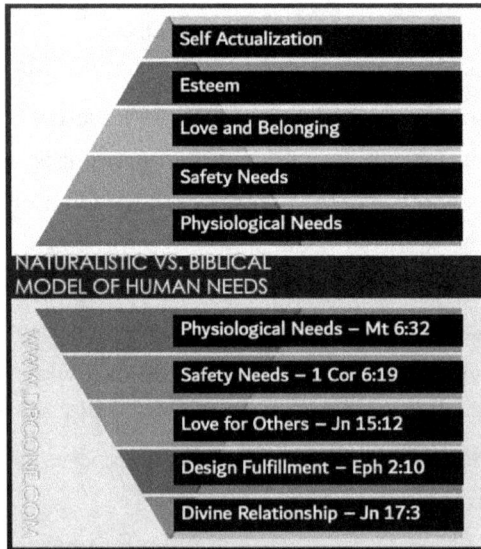

Figure 1: Naturalistic vs. Biblical Model of Human Needs

Once we have that divine relationship a second layer would be design fulfillment. Who are we? What are we designed to do? We are designed to walk in relationship with our Creator, and our Creator has designed us. Ephesians 2:10 says that we are His workmanship. We've been crafted – created in Christ Jesus – for good works, for doing good things, for good deeds. and then it says that He prepared those good deeds beforehand. So we are designed for *that*. Well, what are those good things? If I don't know what those good things are, how can I help someone fulfill their design? And if I'm not helping someone fulfill their design, then I'm a poor leader.

The third component that we need is love for others. Because our Creator is telling us these first two components have to do with (1) your relationship with your Creator and then (2) how He has designed you to fulfill that. The next step in fulfilling that is loving others. I can't be a good person fulfilling good works if I'm not engaging in loving other people, let alone being a leader.

Think about it this way: every religious system and philosophical system on the planet is focused on helping us work our way toward the divine or godlikeness. Biblical Christianity is entirely different than that. The Creator comes to humanity recognizing we can't be like Him on our own, so He provides that for us (through Christ). Relating to the Divine is not by our own working to achieve it, rather it is by faith, by simply trusting Him, and not by our own efforts. Consequently, when we move toward design fulfillment, we recognize that we are already new creatures. Now our focus ought to be on walking in that relationship. Then the next step is loving others. I can't say I love someone I haven't seen if I'm not loving the people He created that I have seen.

After that, we can acknowledge that our safety needs are important. Paul tells his readers in First Corinthians that their bodies are the temple of God. God created them. Their bodies have value and should be cared for. Safety is important. Then physiological needs are important. Meeting those daily, basic things through the lens of our Creator's priorities, we discover that even those basic things have meaning. In Ecclesiastes we are told they have value and they have meaning. Then we recognize that Jesus explains in Matthew 6 that God provides those things. This is a worldview thing, and it's totally flipped from the humanistic model of Abraham Maslow. If we adopt Maslow's model, our leadership model is going to be very different than if we flip Maslow's model and look at a more Biblical model. Our (Biblically shaped) leadership model is again totally different. They don't resemble each other in any way, shape, or form – Maslow's hierarchy versus a transformative hierarchy. We've got to understand and make the core worldview choices before we start to look at a strategic plan or develop a mission. We have to deal with these things. They are unavoidable.

Another issue to think through is the importance of starting with who, not why. Simon Sinek did a TED Talk called "Start with why, not what." He explains that we start with the transcendent purpose. We don't start with "here's our processes" and "here's what we're going to do." As we go back to our hierarchy, we see that the first greatest need that every person has is to be intimate with their Creator, to be in right relationship with their Creator. This gives meaning and identity. This gives us everything we need to conduct the rest of our lives. It seems Sinek misses that. He's suggesting we should work from the why – a transcendent purpose. Yet if we don't understand who we are, who we're designed to be, we certainly cannot understand accurately a transcendent purpose.

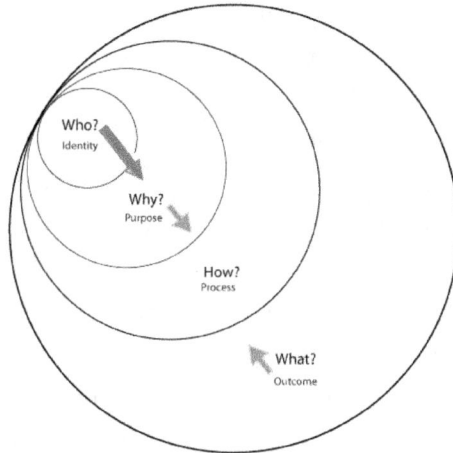

Figure 2: Start with Who

Now we're starting with the who – that's who we are and who we're about. We move out from there. Then we have the why. Then we have that transcendent purpose. Then we get to how. What are the processes that we're going to follow to achieve that? And then we get to the what, which is the outcome. But then that what takes us back again. Once we have that outcome we're not finished. We're still here. We still have activity to do. How do we take the next step once we've achieved an outcome? We have to go back to who are we and who are we designed to be. Then, what's our purpose? So, we start with who, not why.

Sinek uses Apple computers as an example. He'll say that Apple is an example of the transcendent why, that Apple had the purpose of creating these incredible products to change life. But it wasn't really about Apple; it was about a founder's – a creator's – vision. It was about who that creator wanted this entity to be. Not to be too critical of Sinek's approach, but the purpose came from that creator and that founder. We don't start with the why unless we first know *the who*. If I don't know who I am and who's created their priorities in my life, then how can I ever answer the question of why? Recognizing who we are and who we've been designed to be is an important part of a transformative leadership model. In Ephesians 4:1 Paul, after explaining who we are, who our creator is, and who our creator has made us to be, says "I beg you walk in a manner worthy of your calling."

I'm supposed to walk in this manner, and I'm supposed to help lead people through that process for them to be able to walk in a manner worthy of their calling. But it's just worthless in the end if I'm ignoring their identity and their calling and just engaging in transactions with them or strategies with them or working towards only some kind of accomplishment for an institution or an organization. If on the other hand I'm acknowledging these things, and I'm leading someone down that path, then every little thing that we're engaging in, every little policy, and every little strategy matters. Every engagement and every transaction matters. Solomon in his profound book of Ecclesiastes really underscores that whole concept. The book of Ecclesiastes shows how all the great things we may do are meaningless without a God-perspective, but when we engage with God, even the seemingly menial tasks have great meaning and are worthwhile.

Too often we think only institutionally and organizationally. In the context of organizational leadership, it is appropriate to think along those lines, but never *only* along those lines, and certainly not *first* along those lines. Transcendent purpose starts with an individual. It doesn't start with an organization. If we're understanding that the people who are part of this organization have a transcendent purpose (they're designed to be someone; they are someone; and they're designed to do something) then when they engage with the organization, the organization needs to foster their ability to walk in a manner worthy of their calling to fulfill their design. When an organization is taking that approach to leadership, the organization is so much richer because it then becomes a laboratory for personal growth of the individual members of the team. Because each individual is trying to fulfill their own design, that third element of the hierarchy – the loving each other component – makes them tremendous teammates and team members. Transformative leadership is situational. It has got its own hierarchy. It starts with who, not why. It engages a transcendent purpose.

Let's just think through some leadership traits and skills, looking at them through that particular transformative leadership lens. We might say that four basic traits that a leader needs to have are: (1) self-awareness, (2) social awareness, (3) self-management, and (4) social management. Self-awareness, to many, would simply be awareness of our personality, being aware of our tools, being aware of our limitations. those kinds of things. I would suggest there is much more than that. Self-awareness is understanding who I am in the great context of things, understanding who I am designed to be, understanding my Creator. I'm not truly self-aware unless I'm rightly dealing with those things. But if I'm not self-aware, how in the world can I help someone else to be self-aware (which leadership seems to require)?

I've got to be aware of myself. I've also got to be aware of others. I've got to be aware of what's going on with other people. What are the challenges they're facing? What are the advantages they have? I've got to have an awareness of other people not just of myself.

Then there's self-management. Not only do I need to be aware, but I also need to have self-control. I need to be able to manage my thoughts, actions, behaviors, speech, etc. If I can't do that, I'm not going to be a very effective leader. Social management considers how I engage in relationships with others. How do I manage those interactions with people? Perhaps by now you can recognize the essential pattern: I must deal with myself. I must deal with others. I must be aware of myself. I must be aware of others. If I can't do those four things or I don't have those four things, I'm simply not going to be effective in in leadership.

## SKILLS

Let's look at some skills and apply those traits in more specific expressions. *Primal Leadership* by Goleman and Boyatzis and McKee that deals with a number of these. And we could add fifty more to the list. I'm just going to present a few of these to help us think through what it means to be a transformative leader. Some have been adapted to better fit our context:

- **Self-evaluation** - I have to be able to evaluate myself accurately. How do I do that? What is the basis for the grid or the standard used? From a worldview perspective, if I don't understand what I'm designed to be then I can't accurately evaluate myself. We don't evaluate and assess well unless we have a standard or a point of reference. Consider an example. If I give you a test, challenging you to answer questions with A, B, or C., what standard should you look at to know the answer? In this example, there is no standard. You're just going to take the test. Well, that would obviously be an absurd waste of time. We don't do that in any aspect of life unless we're trying to understand where a person is, perhaps, in a survey of some kind. There's got to be a standard whereby I can evaluate myself. That is a core worldview issue and impacts every area of our lives – including how we lead.

- **Personal Growth and Discipline** - If I'm not committed to my own personal growth and I don't have the discipline to work through the necessary steps, then I don't have the skill. Personal growth is critical, and it fits right in line with the transformative concept because personal growth is what transformation is all about.

- **Cultural Exegesis -** To be able to exegete the culture – draw out what's happening – is important. This is part of that social awareness. If I'm not familiar with what's happening, it's hard to lead people who are in the midst of those cultural developments. I need to know where they are. I need to know what's happening.

- **Critical Thinking and Analysis -** I need to be skilled at critical thinking and analysis.

- **Collaboration -** I need to be able to collaborate – work with the team, work with others – not simply direct them to needed tasks.

- **Research -** I need to be able to do research at a high level. I need to be able to acquire data and process data.

- **Public Speaking and Persuasive Reasoning -** I need to have some capacity in public speaking and persuasive reasoning. If I can't communicate, if I can't persuade (essentially selling is persuading), I won't be an effective leader.

- **Counseling and Receiving Counsel -** I've got to be able to communicate with others and reprove and challenge and encourage and build up. And I've got to be able to receive those things from others.

- **Data Analysis -** Data analysis related to research doesn't do me much good if I simply acquire data, but can't or don't do anything with that data. It's a little overwhelming I'll admit because the data that we have in our generation – the tools for data generation – is amazing. We have got to develop the skills of analyzing and then implementing those results.

- **Implementation** is an important aspect as well. Putting new information into practice is an important part of personal growth and leading others

- **Emotional Intelligence Resulting in Either Resonance or Dissonance** – Goldman et al suggest that EI (emotional intelligence) will result in either resonance or dissonance. Think in terms of music. Dissonant sound or cacophony is usually fairly awful and generally not effective for accomplishing anything positive (there are exceptions, of course). Resonance is broadcasting to all and is a unifying factor. All are receiving it and hearing it. Emotional intelligence plays into that. I would simply define emotional intelligence as *character*. When Paul told the Roman believers to rejoice with those who rejoice and weep with those who weep, that's an aspect of emotional intelligence. It's the idea of being able to interact with the person where that person is in the context that person finds themselves. It is being aware of who that person really is, their context, and being able to engage with them on *that* ground rather than on my own ground.

- **Conflict Resolution** – Involves being able to understand conflict, understand what's causing conflict, and understand motivations. Resolution entails engaging the parties involved and helping to lead them to a resolution. If the conflict cannot be resolved, then it is important to be capable to manage it and sustain the culture despite the conflict. Conflict isn't necessarily a bad thing. It can be a catalyst for growth.

- **Resource Management** – Understand what resources are available and how to use them, allocating them properly.

- **Networking** – Be able to communicate with others. Build relationships.

- **Use of Media** – Use tools for communicating. This is very similar to the public speaking and persuasive reasoning skill. It's just a different context. Everybody's a public speaker, some just do it on social media and perhaps not very effectively.

## ORGANIZATIONAL LIFECYCLES AND LEADERSHIP NEEDS

We'll also want to think about organizational life cycles and leadership needs. Organizations have lifecycles. We can't make it all about the organization. Organizations rise and fall, and that is appropriate. We need to understand what those lifecycles are and then what needs there are during those various stages. In this context I like to borrow Paul's approach when he discusses human growth and development in terms of (1) infancy, (2) childhood, (3) adolescence, and (4) maturity. Infancy in an organizational setting would be development and launch. Childhood would be the growth and development stage of the organization. Adolescence would represent the greatest era of change. As it has been launched, it may experience a period of rapid growth. Change and development is needed to make continued growth sustainable. Then the organization moves through that period of change into maturity. During the maturity phase there might be various crises that have to be encountered and addressed. There are times innovation is especially needed. We must then develop the next generation of leaders to carry on the organization or to end that organization and create a new organization.

Let's consider some of the tools needed. In infancy – in that development and launch stage – you need some vision. Somebody's got to be saying this is what this person could be, or this is what this organization can be. There has to be deliberateness to develop the tools and processes to at least start walking in that direction. There has to be clarity and goals otherwise a person doesn't know what the milestones are that we're trying to hit on the way to fulfilling that vision. This also requires great patience and training on the part of leaders. It's slow. It's difficult. We are building something from nothing, in a sense, and if we don't exhibit great patience and understanding as people try to understand for themselves what is happening (and what needs to happen) then we can't lead well.

In the next stage, childhood/growth and development, some things are established. You are moving forward toward the accomplishment of the mission, and toward the fulfillment of the vision. Responsiveness is needed on processes. There will be much feedback given. Much assessment and adjustment. Some of those adjustments will work. Some will not. They have to be refined. We **(1) have to be responsive on processes**. In other words if we are *governed* by processes, then the organization will be stunted and will likely stay in childhood. It will never even move to adolescence. Many businesses and organizations stay focused only on processes and process enforcement and are not responsive to change where change is needed.

An organization **(2) must be able to address and resolve conflict**. You can sometimes get through infancy – through those early exciting stages – without conflict. It can be awesome. Everybody's on the same page and things are moving along briskly. But then when things start to grow rapidly, people get too stretched. We might realize some processes work terribly and they have to be changed. But only some of the people may see it. Because you're not responsive on the processes, conflicts will arise and if they are not addressed or resolved at that stage, the organization (in part due to our failure) is stuck in childhood.

We have to **(3) develop skill in delegation and accountability** and to be working with other leaders helping them to develop and giving them accountabilities. If we're not, we're stuck in childhood. We have to **(4) foster collaboration,** ensuring that teams are encouraged and people have the tools they need to work together. When we do **these four things** effectively (and there may be others you might add to the list) the organization is better able to move on to adolescence.

The challenge to remember is that adolescence is a period of great change, traumatic and sometimes catastrophic change. We should have grown past a single-leader model by this point, but if we have not, then it is time to make certain that we have got participative and empowering leadership. We've got to have other leaders who are involved. They are empowered because we're now in full on change-management mode. We have to have a team of leaders who can guide others through those murky waters. We have to constantly be restating and reassuring of the vision, mission, and goals. If we're not restating those they will certainly get lost. Amidst all that change we're searching for identity.

Think of it from a personal development perspective. You understand that a thirteen-year-old is going through all kinds of challenges. They don't look like they looked a couple of years ago. They don't feel like they felt. They are identifying themselves differently, and if they're not reassured of their identity they can easily get lost. It works the same way with the organization. At this point there has to be delegation of leadership roles. Not only then do we have an empowered leadership team but now we are delegating the leadership roles. At this point, as the organization nears the end of adolescence, as leaders we should have developed people who can replace us. We can now step aside and let this new generation of leadership handle the maturity stage. If we haven't equipped new leadership then the organization is probably stuck in childhood somewhere. Or perhaps you've gotten an offer to move on or to sell and you've gone and left the organization and *your team* in adolescence to drift back into infancy. The idea of agile leadership is helping to guide the organization through adolescence and change. You've got to have agility. You can't be so focused on processes – on the tools. Tools change. Everything changes, and if we're not adaptive to that, we're stuck in adolescence.

During the stage of maturity, among the successes we encounter, there will arise all kinds of crises that we have to address. We should be pressing on to new innovations, and we should be developing leaders, not necessarily in that order – it hits you when it hits you.

We need to be **reinforcing culture.** Constantly go back to the basics. Recall Vince Lombardi's famous coaching moment. He holds up a football, and he says to these professional football players who have been champions, who have been playing for years, "this is a football." The point is, we're going back to basics. We're going to reinforce the culture. Look at writers like Paul and Peter. They're always constantly taking people back to who they are, who they are designed to be, before they tell a person to do anything. Before they call us to behave this way or walk this way or think this way, they're going to remind us of who we are. Once we understand who we are, now we should think this way. This is who we are; we should talk this way. This is who we are; we should act this way. Continually reinforce the culture.

We ought to **ensure and reward the motivation** of all stakeholders. We ought to make certain that people who have invested to this point – who have brought this entity from infancy to childhood to adolescence and now to maturity – that we have invested in them. How dare we as leaders allow someone to carry the load and bring the institution or the organization to this point without making sure they're blessed. We need to ensure that the reasons they got into this in the first place are being fulfilled.

Then we've got to **exercise agility**. That's just ongoing. Always be able to adapt because identity doesn't change. Ultimate purpose doesn't change but how we get there, there's a lot of change needed.

We need to continually be **promoting innovation** and new models. Vision and mission generally don't change for an organization. They can, but generally won't. But the processes and procedures and models to pave the path to mission and vision fulfillment do. Those things change so we need to be looking at how to innovate, how to have better processes, better ways to move forward, better models.

There has to be **accountability and assessment** at every level. Accountability needs to be data driven and based on actual assessments – ways that you can objectively determine what's being accomplished, what's being fulfilled.

We need to be deliberate, fostering **delegation for development.** We need to be prepared for and actually beginning the process of handing the baton to the next generation Sometimes (not always) that means stepping out of the way. What it means is you're building something essentially from infancy to maturity, and when it gets to the maturity, sometimes the best way to lead is to step aside. But we generally aren't willing to do that. Too often we think "well I got us here; I'm going to keep on." That can stunt the leaders that you have empowered in delegating, and oftentimes then they're going to be squelched and have to go somewhere else. Maybe you provide them opportunities to go elsewhere so they can start the process of acquiring that equipping. I would encourage leaders not to try to hold on to leadership or we will sometimes not allow your organization to hit maturity. We might hinder our team in their personal development. That certainly doesn't mean we can't be a good leader who stays in a role for many years. It just means that a leader's focus ought not to be holding onto leadership. Rather it ought to be investing in others so that they will be equipped to lead.

# 2
# DON'T START WITH *WHY,*
# START WITH *WHO*

In seeking to identify the seeds of excellence, one popular approach traces the beginnings of excellence back to the question *Why?*[1] In this model, we could critique a more common alternative of beginning with the outcome (the *What*) and arriving at the *Why*, rather than beginning with the *Why*. In this model, the idea is that before arriving at the process (*How*) and the outcome (*What*), it is of primary importance that we solidify the *Why*.

In a way the concept corresponds to reality, however, there is a key piece missing. This model lacks the worldview follow-through to really work. To illustrate, in explaining the model, Simon Sinek suggests that Apple does not work from the *What*, but rather that they work from the *Why*. Their greatness lies in their ability to inspire based on the *Why*. But I would suggest that Steve Jobs had something to do with that, and Apple's success emanated first from *who he was* than from *why* he created the ideas and products that he did. If we focus on the *Why*, we are missing the priority.

Look at it this way. In the Biblical worldview, we see illustrated the clear concept that identity and origin give rise to purpose. We could say that ontology (existence) precedes teleology (design), or at least that teleology is ordered by ontology. Colossians 1:16 concludes with the statement that "all things were created by Him and for Him." The fact

---

[1] Simon Sinek, *Start With Why* (Portfolio, 2009).

that He created gives Him authority over all that He created, and demonstrates evidence that He has authority over that which He created. Ontology leads to teleology. This is why His calming the storm was such a big deal – He had the authority to do that, and that meant something significant about who He was.[2] Here's another example from Galatians 2:20:

> I have been crucified with Christ; and it is no longer I who live, but Christ lives in me; and the *life* which I now live in the flesh I live by faith in the Son of God, who loved me and gave Himself up for me.

For those who have believed in Christ, their identity has changed. Who they are is now so wrapped up in Christ, that their actions should be – are designed to be – reflective of their identity. Paul put it perfectly when he exhorted believers to "walk in a manner worthy of the calling with which you have been called."[3] He adds, "for you were formerly darkness, but now you are Light in the Lord; walk as children of Light."[4] *Identity determines design and purpose.*

In the famous dialogue between Nicodemus and Jesus, Nicodemus recognized that the *What* and the *How* emanated from Jesus' identity. He wanted to verify who Jesus was. Perhaps to understand the *Why*, Nicodemus introduced his questions with the comment, "Rabbi, we know that You have come from God *as* a teacher; for no one can do these signs that You do unless God is with him."[5] Jesus responds to the

---

[2] Matthew 8:23-27.
[3] Ephesians 4:1.
[4] Ephesians 5:8.
[5] John 3:2.

*Why* question with the *How*: "Truly, truly, I say to you, unless one is born again he cannot see the kingdom of God.[6]" Nicodemus's questioning focused on the *How* and the *What*, but Jesus ultimately turned Nicodemus's focus to the *Who*: the object of faith is Christ, Himself. He explained that because He was who He was, He had a purpose to fulfill (including providing for the salvation of humanity), He had a method for doing that (paying the price as a substitution for fallen humanity), and the outcome was eternal life. The first and most important piece of the entire discussion and process was the identity of Jesus Christ.

The Biblical worldview is transparently focused on the idea that identity is a key starting point. God appeals to His own identity in communicating the greatness of His holiness, sovereignty, grace, love, etc. God appeals to our identity in challenging us to excellence. So, when we are seeking the proper understanding of *Why* we should be what we should be, we have to start with *Who* He is, and *Who* He has made us to be. Know who He is, know who you are, and the *why*, *how*, and *what* will begin to make a lot more sense and be much more accessible.

---

[6] John 3:2.

# 3
# DEFINING SUCCESS

Do an online search for the phrase "What is success?" and you may get around 1.13 billion results. Much has been said about success. Everybody seems to want it, but it is surprising how few actually can define it. Success is commonly defined as the achieving of an aim or purpose. To some it is the attainment of popularity or profit. A successful person is often perceived, then, as someone who achieves desired aims or prospers in their endeavors. But what should be the aim or purpose? And how do we define prosperity?

A popular meme suggests that success changes with age:

At age 4 success is not peeing in your pants.
At age 6 success is finding your way home from school.
At age 16 success is having a driver's license.
From age 17-64 success is having money and friends.
At age 65 success is keeping a driver's license.
At age 75 success is finding your way home from anywhere.
At age 80 success is not peeing in your pants.

Others make more serious attempts at defining success. Zig Ziglar asserts that, "Success means doing the best we can with what we have...reaching for the highest that is in us, becoming all that we can be."[1] But to know what is best, don't we have to know what is good? And highest *what*? Did Hitler reach pretty high? Or not? How do we

---

[1] http://www.incomediary.com/50-great-thoughts-on-success.

measure? Winston Churchill is purported to have said that, "Success is going from failure to failure without losing enthusiasm." Enthusiasm. But why should I be enthusiastic about anything? Especially in the midst of repeated failure. And what is failure anyway? How can I know what that is until I know what success is? Maya Angelou observed that "Success is liking yourself, liking what you do, and liking how you do it."[2] Liking stuff. So "I" am the judge of success. If I am easily amused, apparently, I have a great chance to be successful. Bessie A. Stanley said, in a quote often attributed to Ralph Waldo Emerson, that success is to

> laugh often and much, to win the respect of intelligent people and the affection of children, to earn the appreciation of honest critics and endure the betrayal of false friends, to appreciate beauty, to find the best in others, to leave the world a bit better, whether by a healthy child, a garden patch, or a redeemed social condition; to know even one life has breathed easier because you have lived. This is to have succeeded![3]

I don't even know where to start with this one. I guess we need some fake friends to betray us, and we need to start a garden. Legendary UCLA basketball coach John Wooden said that, "Success is peace of mind, which is a direct result of self-satisfaction in knowing you did your best to become the best you are capable of becoming."[4] Again, what is best, what is good? Did you ever know someone who had total peace of

---

[2] Quoted in Michael Garrett, "Maya Angelou in Her Own Words," *Success.com*, September 19, 2011, viewed at https://www.success.com/maya-angelou-in-her-own-words/.
[3] Chris Hanlon, "On Fake Emerson Quotes," August 27, 2019, viewed at https://avidly.lareviewofbooks.org/2019/08/27/on-fake-emerson-quotes/.
[4] John Wooden, *Wooden* (Contemporary Books, 1997), 170.

mind, and were satisfied with themselves, that they had done their best to become their best...and yet they were totally incompetent? Peace of mind can be deceptive. Thomas Edison is credited famously with saying that "Success is 1% inspiration, 99% perspiration."[5] He tells us how to achieve success but not what it is. All we know is the road to success is sweaty and probably smells bad, but we don't know where that road leads. Stephen Covey suggests we make our own definition: "If you carefully consider what you want to be said of you in the funeral experience, you will find your definition of success."[6] In short, what others think of you defines your success, and you won't know if you did it right or wrong until you are dead – and that's only if you show up for your funeral. On time. Deepak Chopra posits that "Success in life could be defined as the continued expansion of happiness and progressive realization of worthy goals."[7] Chopra suggests the recipe for success includes two things: happiness – but only if it is continually expanding (bummer if it stops), and realization of worthy goals. Great, but what makes something *worthy*?

It is remarkable that these brilliant people are really leading us nowhere. Of course, there are some magnificent grains of truth in these comments – more in some than others – but none of them have captured what real success is. You know what every single one of the above definitions of success is missing? *An actual definition of success.* Each tells us something *about* success – something about how to pursue or how to persevere. But none offers any definition of our purpose and

---

[5] https://www.brainpickings.org/index.php/2013/05/22/manage-your-day-to-day-99u/.

[6] http://www.nytimes.com/2012/07/17/business/stephen-r-covey-herald-of-good-habits-dies-at-79.html?_r=0.

[7] Deepak Chopra, *The Seven Spiritual Laws of Success* (Amber-Allen Publishing, 2015), 4.

how we can measure it. Solomon illustrates the hopelessness of this when he talks about the emptiness of life without God – the lack of purpose, the heartache of insignificance: "For who knows what is good for a man during *his* lifetime, *during* the few years of his futile life? He will spend them like a shadow. For who can tell a man what will be after him under the sun?"[8] There is an inherent challenge in understanding what is good (therefore what is best), and we need some help. God provides that. OK, now it is God's turn. Let's see if God offers us a better definition of success. He starts by telling us that we are new creations with a purpose: "For by grace you have been saved through faith; and that not of yourselves, *it is* the gift of God; not as a result of works, so that no one may boast. For we are His workmanship, created in Christ Jesus for good works, which God prepared beforehand so that we would walk in them."[9] We are new creations with a purpose – good works. What are good works? Since He is the designer, He gets to define. "He has told you, O man, what is good (tov); And what does the LORD require of you but to do justice (*mishpat*), to love kindness (*chessed*), And to walk humbly with (*im*) your God (*elohika*)."[10] In short:

> What you do (justice, judgment, rightness).
> What you love (kindness, goodness).
> How you walk (humbly).
> Who you walk with (your God).

The *good* for humanity is faithfulness in deed, affection, humility, and relationship. Consider this practical example from Luke 10:38-42.

---

[8] Ecclesiastes 6:12.
[9] Ephesians 2:8-10.
[10] Micah 6:8.

Now as they were traveling along, He entered a village; and a woman named Martha welcomed Him into her home. She had a sister called Mary, **who was seated at the Lord's feet, listening to His word**. But Martha was distracted with all her preparations; and she came up *to Him* and said, "Lord, do You not care that my sister has left me to do all the serving alone? Then tell her to help me." But the Lord answered and said to her, "Martha, Martha, you are worried and bothered about so many things; but *only* one thing is necessary, for **Mary has chosen the good part, which shall not be taken away from her.**"

You want real success? *Lasting success?* Mary figured out the formula. She simply walked humbly with her God. Success isn't determined by dollars, friends (or social media followers), or accomplishments. Success can't be measured by scores, stat lines, good grades, or even dry pants. Success is faithfulness in deed, affection, humility, and relationship with Him. It is doing justice, or rightness, as defined by God. It is about setting your heart on what God values. It is about walking with humility. Success is ultimately walking with God, not simply for Him or about Him, but *with* Him. As you look back on your endeavors, I pray that you will measure it not just in terms of what you did, but whether or not you did it *with* God.

*4*

# HOW TO FAIL WELL:
## A MATRIX FOR PRIORITIZATION

As I stand in front of leadership students at the beginning of a class, I write on a whiteboard four words in no particular order: children, God, ministry, and spouse. I ask them a simple question:

"Are any of you perfect?"

My absurd question is met with the smirks and snickers it deserves.

"So you are going to fail somewhere along the line, right?"

More smirks. Not so many snickers.

"So pick one. Where are you going to fail? Are you going to fail as a father to your children? Are you going to fail in your relationship with God? Are you going to fail as a husband? Or will you fail in your ministry role or career?"

The smirks are gone now, replaced with pained looks of concern. The reality of the challenge of priorities is beginning to hit home.

Paul Vitello paints a disturbing picture: "Members of the clergy now suffer from obesity, hypertension, and depression *at rates higher than most Americans*. In the last decade, their use of antidepressants has risen, while their life expectancy has fallen. Many would change jobs if they could."[1] Add to that a fifty percent divorce rate among pastors, and an average career lifespan of less than five years, and one might begin to wonder if pastoral ministry should be avoided altogether.

Paul explains in 1 Timothy 3:1 that the role of oversight in the church (equated with pastoring in Acts 20:28) is a fine thing to desire. *Desire.* But who would desire what Vitello described? Well, simply put, we are often doing ministry *wrong*, and we pay a heavy price for it. Inevitably some respond to my question something like, "Well, I can't fail in my ministry, because people are depending on me. And I can't fail with my kids; they need me too much. And I shouldn't fail with God, but I suppose He will understand if I did. I guess I will either fail with God or my relationship to my spouse; perhaps they will understand and can handle it." The problem here is a simple matter of priorities. Consider this scenario: you only have enough time for three things, but you have four things on which you must focus – (again, in no particular order) children, God, ministry, spouse. Some might suggest choosing to do all four at a lesser capacity, simply to make an attempt at all four. But let's take a look at the Biblical perspective to see if that works.

Jesus describes the meaning of life in John 17:3 – to know God, to have a relationship with God. Further, He reminds us of the importance of loving God above all else,[2] and the centrality of abiding in Him.[3] Valuing anything – even family[4] – over Him is counted as idolatry. There is simply no room for disregarding our relationship with

---

[1] Paul Vitello, "Taking a Break From the Lord's Work" *New York Times*, August 1, 2010, viewed at
https://www.nytimes.com/2010/08/02/nyregion/02burnout.html?pagewanted=1&_r=2&hp&.
[2] Matthew 6:24, 22:37.
[3] John 15.
[4] Luke 14:26.

Him unless we miss the entire point in our lives. We cannot place our relationship with Him in second place to anything.

We have also been given specific instructions regarding how to treat the woman who has given herself and whom God has given. Husbands are to love their wives as Christ loved the church, having given Himself up for her.[5] The husband's love is to illustrate that of Christ. What a lofty standard, indeed. Peter adds, "You husbands live with your wives in an understanding way...show her honor as a fellow heir of the grace of life, so that your prayers will not be hindered."[6] Remarkable. If husbands aren't treating their wives as they ought to be, their fellowship with God is hindered. I can't maintain proper fellowship with Him if I am not maintaining proper fellowship with my fellow heir. Clearly, in assessing personal priorities, there is no room for disregarding the marital relationship. Failure is simply not an option unless we are ready for some very painful consequences.

As for our children, we have clear instructions there too. Fathers, for example, are commanded to nourish them in the discipline and instruction of the Lord.[7] In that same passage fathers are commanded not to incite their children to wrath. Pastors (and other leaders) have been so bad in this regard that "preacher's kid" has become a synonym for one who is rebellious and bitter. How tragic. Instead, our children should be recipients of our love and grace. They should know our undying love. They should have our quantity, and not be stuck with the scraps we so disingenuously try to label "quality." These are the most dependent and most helpless of the flock – young disciples needing shepherding. If we fail there, we cause our children to

---

[5] Ephesians 5:25.
[6] 1 Peter 3:7.
[7] Ephesians 6:4.

stumble badly and in ways that are difficult to overcome. What could be worse than for a father to be a stumbling block for his own children? Jesus puts it bluntly: "It is inevitable that stumbling blocks come, but woe to him through whom they come. It would be better for him if a millstone were hung around his neck and he were thrown into the sea, than that he would cause one of these little ones to stumble."[8] Nope. There is no way we can de-prioritize our own children. Not when they are this important to Him, and not when He has given fathers primary responsibility for them.

So where does that leave us? Our relationship with God is priority one. Our marital relationship is vitally important to Him, as is our relationship with our children. We aren't given the option of failing in any of these areas. Thankfully, He is gracious when we do fail (and of course we do). But even though there is no condemnation for those in Christ Jesus,[9] He still allows us sometimes to deal with the consequences of our poor priorities. While these personal relationships are important, so are our other ministry responsibilities. However, all too often we overestimate those priorities. That's right – *we make them bigger than they really are*. We are not the Good Shepherd. He is.[10] We are not building the church. He is.[11] We do not equip the saints for the work of service. His word does.[12]  We aren't responsible to do singlehandedly the work of service. The whole church is.[13] It is not my church or your church. It is His church.[14] It is no different with careers or other endeavors of

---

8 Luke 17:1-2.
9 Romans 8:1.
10 John 10:11.
11 Matthew 16:18.
12 Ephesians 4:12, 2 Timothy 3:17.
13 Ephesians 4:12, 1 Corinthians 12:12-27.
14 Matthew 16:18.

those not necessarily leading in a formal ministry setting. Unless He builds the house, it doesn't get built.[15] Get the point? A central reason for leadership failure is we simply make the job bigger than it is, either by internal or external pressures. Instead, we should look to the One who wrote the job descriptions, and work within the structure He provided.

After some Biblical verification and thoughtful soul searching, the class all agrees that the whiteboard should reflect the Biblical order of our priorities: God, spouse, children, ministry. But the implications of that prioritization have to be emphasized. No leader is perfect. Every leader will encounter failure – and fairly often. But he must be unwilling to fail in his relationships (as God defines them) to God, spouse, and children. By process of elimination, *that means that he must be ready to accept failure in meeting the demands of career and (external) ministry.* That does not mean he can mishandle God's word or violate the job description God has put in place (for those things affect the relationship with Him). It simply means that God has designed leadership roles to work in concert with the other priority relationships He has established. He has not put leaders in a no-win situation. We do that to ourselves when we add to His job description. Let's simplify. Examine the Scriptures to define the leadership roles, and let the roles go no further, lest they infringe on other Biblical priorities.

In short, a pastor who is unwilling to fail as a pastor (in the context of extra-Biblical expectations) has absolutely no business being a pastor. He is attempting to do the impossible, and he will fail – probably publicly and catastrophically. On the other hand, a pastor who is willing to accept failure in ministry outside of those three relationships

---

[15] Psalm 127:1-3.

(God, wife, children) has a chance to excel in that ministry. How then should we avoid failure in ministry? I suggest we shouldn't avoid it at all. Just make sure we are failing well and failing in the right areas. The same principles apply to leaders in any setting: Biblical priorities are the bedrock of success in any leadership role.

# 5
# GREAT AS THE ENEMY OF GOOD:
## IF IT'S WORTH DOING, IT'S WORTH DOING... POORLY

A wise man once told me "If it's worth doing, it's worth doing poorly." Though I cannot recall the context of the conversation, I have never forgotten those words. They serve as a lasting reminder to me not to trade good for excellent. Sometimes we can get so caught up in pursuing excellence that we become too fearful of mediocrity to even make an attempt. Mediocrity isn't all bad, and from mediocrity sometimes excellence can emerge when we least expect it.

For example, I frequently encounter students who are struggling with the overload that comes with higher education. Many struggle to the point of dropping out because they aren't able to meet their studies with the degree of success to which they have become accustomed in other areas of life. To folks like these, I say, "If it's worth doing, it's worth doing poorly." So, you get a C instead of an A. GPA isn't everything – in fact, a graduate degree with a low GPA beats an undergraduate degree with a high GPA every time. Just do your best and make progress. A little progress is better than no progress. Whether it is in education or any other pursuit, it seems far better to make an attempt than to never engage for fear of mediocrity or even failure. Even failure isn't always bad. Ask Thomas Edison.

The apostle Paul was a tentmaker,[1] and I would bet he was probably a very good one. But I would also wager he wasn't nearly as good as he could have been. Why? Because he had other priorities and he spent his time largely on those priorities (e.g., proclaiming the word of God and teaching it to everyone who would listen). Tent making was important to Paul, but it wasn't worth all of his time. He was able to assess how to spend his time and limit his tent making efforts to the point that they complemented his other ministry. I would suppose that he was as good a tent maker as he needed to be. Obviously, we should always prefer excellence, but sometimes not good enough is actually good enough.

---

[1] Acts 18:3.

# 6
# WHY DO EXCELLENT WORK?
## A WORKER'S MANIFESTO

I once heard a story – I don't recall where – of a builder who was commissioned by his employer to build a house. The builder's employer gave specific instructions regarding the quality of the house. He wanted it to be excellent, but the builder tried to save money and effort for himself by cutting corners. The builder knew that he could hide his below-par craftsmanship so that it wouldn't be discovered until years later. In the end, the house looked good, but the low quality of the building left much to be desired. When the house was completed, the employer who owned the house handed the keys to the builder and explained that he wanted to give the house to the builder as a show of gratitude for many years of service. Of course, the builder instantly regretted his laziness and poor workmanship.

The moral of that story seems to be that we should do excellent work because we never know when we might personally benefit. In a way, there is some truth to that, because the Bible does present that the expectation of reward is a legitimate motivation for good work. The worker is worthy of his wages.[1] God is a rewarder of those who seek Him.[2] Jesus even uses the concept of reward in one of His final

---

[1] Luke 10:7, 1 Timothy 5:18.
[2] Hebrews 11:6.

Scriptural exhortations.[3] Paul explains that those who are working for others should always remember that they are, in fact, working for the Lord, and that the ultimate reward comes from Him:

> Whatever you do, do your work heartily, as for the Lord rather than for men, knowing that from the Lord you will receive the reward of the inheritance. It is the Lord Christ whom you serve.[4]

Reward is certainly a legitimate motivation, but there is perhaps a greater motivation still. We are reminded that "Whatever you do in word or deed, *do* all in the name of the Lord Jesus, giving thanks through Him to God the Father."[5] There is something special about working in the name of Jesus – meaning that we are working as if directly for Him, accomplishing what He would want accomplished. Paul identifies the significance of this in 1 Corinthians 10:31, "Whether, then, you eat or drink or whatever you do, do all to the glory of God." We should be seeking His glorification.

The motivation comes from loving Him because He first loved us.[6] If His purpose is to glorify Himself (or to express His character through His creation, much like artists express themselves through their craft), then our own loving response to Him would be to serve that purpose. We should want Him to be glorified, and should find gratification when He is glorified.

---

[3] Revelation 22:12.
[4] Colossians 3:23-24.
[5] Colossians 3:17.
[6] 1 John 4:19.

Notice also how desiring to glorify Him is related to gratitude. Psalm 86:12 says, "I will give thanks to you, O Lord my God, with all my heart, and will glorify Your name forever." We see the same thing in Colossians 3:17. In these contexts, we are glorifying Him because of what He has already done for us, not simply because of something He will do in the future (i.e., future rewards). Ultimately, we ought to want Him to be glorified because "to Him belong glory and dominion."[7] It is rightfully His, and if we love Him we ought to want for Him what is rightfully His.

Our work matters to God. What we do can and should result in His glory: with our good behavior,[8] with our obedience,[9] with our bodies,[10] and with our work.[11] Of course we can never work to earn good standing with God – He has already provided that by grace through faith in Christ,[12] but "we are His workmanship created in Christ Jesus for good works which He prepared beforehand so that we would walk in them."[13] He has laid before us a path of excellence in all that we do. Being committed to excellence in our labor should be more than a slogan to us because we have significant reasons to be excellent.

Finally then, brethren, we request and exhort you in the Lord Jesus, that as you received from us *instruction* as to how you

---

[7] 1 Peter 4:11.
[8] 1 Peter 2:12.
[9] 2 Corinthians 9:12.
[10] 1 Corinthians 6:20.
[11] Colossians 3:23-24.
[12] Ephesians 2:8-9.
[13] Ephesians 2:10.

ought to walk and please God (just as you actually do walk), that you **excel still more.**"[14]

---

[14] 1 Thessalonians 4:1.

7

# PRIORITIZATION AND TIME MANAGEMENT

According to the Bureau of Labor Statistics, American Time Use Survey (2012), the average working person between the ages of 25-54 spends 2.5 hours per workday in leisure and sports. (Is Facebook a sport)?  That's 12.5 hours per week, about 50 hours per month, and roughly 600 hours per year. And note – that does not include weekends! While we certainly need rest and recharging for the many tasks God provides, perhaps we can ask ourselves what we are doing with those 600 hours per year.

### Time use on an average work day for employed persons ages 25 to 54 with children

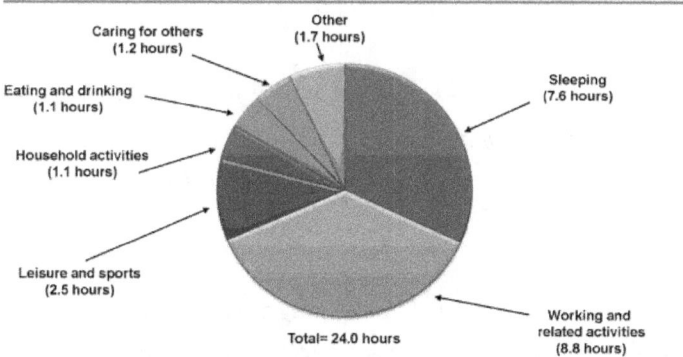

Caring for others
(1.2 hours)

Other
(1.7 hours)

Eating and drinking
(1.1 hours)

Sleeping
(7.6 hours)

Household activities
(1.1 hours)

Leisure and sports
(2.5 hours)

Working and
related activities
(8.8 hours)

Total= 24.0 hours

NOTE: Data include employed persons on days they worked, ages 25 to 54, who lived in households with children under 18. Data include non-holiday weekdays and are annual averages for 2011. Data include related travel for each activity.

SOURCE: Bureau of Labor Statistics, American Time Use Survey

Figure 3: American Time Use Survey

Consider some of these estimates:

> To learn a new language in a year – 30 minutes per day (182 hours in a year)
> To walk across the continental United States – 180 minutes per day (1100 hours in a year)
> To learn how to fly and obtain a Private Pilot certificate – an average of 20 minutes per day (120 hours in a year)
> To read through the Bible once in a year (at a comfortable pace) – 20 minutes per day (120 hours in a year)

These numbers are a bit shocking, right? Especially in relation to the 600 hours that we spend doing…well, pretty much nothing. As we consider our frustration and disappointment over the time we have wasted, let's consider three passages that help us think Biblically about how we can use our time in the future.

## ISAIAH 28:9-10

*"To whom would He teach knowledge, And to whom would He interpret the message? Those just weaned from milk? Those just taken from the breast? "For He says, 'Order on order, order on order, Line on line, line on line, A little here, a little there.' "*

In the context of God's judgment on Israel, this passage considers God's method of speaking to the rebellious nation. He would teach them simply – like children, yet the nation would not listen. So, whereas we would normally teach "Order on order, order on order, Line on line, line on line, A little here, a little there" in order to be understood,

He would teach in that manner, but would not be understood or heeded.[1]

Still the principle of "Order on order, order on order, Line on line, line on line, A little here, a little there" is very helpful. When we prepare a meal, we don't try to make the whole thing at once, rather we prepare each ingredient one at a time. When one writes a book, they don't write the whole thing all at once, but rather one letter, one word, one sentence, and then one paragraph at a time. One doesn't attain fifty years of marriage overnight – it takes fifty years of *one moment at a time.* Parents don't raise children all at once, it takes years full of *moments.* When we learn God's word, we don't learn it all at once, we learn it bit by bit – order on order, line on line, a little here, a little there.

In this same way, if we use the time God has given us with the understanding that it is not one big block of time, but rather many small bits of time, we can be more patient about results. It is important for us to realize that God has given us only the small bits to work with – and we don't know how many of those we have, so we should use them wisely. Life is like a pizza. When we try to devour it all at once, the results are…well…messy and usually disappointing. But when we simply try to use each moment for His glory, things turn out quite differently, and usually we don't need so many napkins.

## PROVERBS 3:5-6

*Trust in the Lord with all your heart And do not lean on your own understanding. In all your ways acknowledge Him, And He will make your paths straight.*

---

[1] Isaiah 28:12.

A straight path is vital for any efficient use of time. When we lean upon our own understanding, the paths start to become crooked and much, much longer. But if we trust in Him, and acknowledge Him in all of our ways, He will make our paths straight. Often, we think that the big things are important to God, but the little things aren't. But if it is true that God does all things for His own glory, then that includes the little things as well. In fact, it is rather arrogant of us to think we can determine which things are important to God and which things aren't. So rather than just trusting Him in the big things and making our own way in the little things, it is so much better to acknowledge Him in all our ways – big and little. Perhaps you are familiar with the exhortation, "Don't sweat the small stuff." Well, there's really no such thing as small stuff. So, let's not sweat the small stuff or the big stuff. If we acknowledge Him in all the stuff, the stuff just works out better.

Additionally – and more importantly – we find ourselves spending the small moments with Him, rather than trying to set aside big blocks of time to get on our knees and pray. And if we begin to spend all of our small moments with Him, it is then that (in my estimation) we begin to really understand what Paul meant when He said "Pray without ceasing."[2] Life is full of small moments and we can spend them with Him or without Him. I can say with certainty a moment with Him has never been wasted.

## MATTHEW 6:19-21

*"Do not store up for yourselves treasures on earth, where moth and rust destroy, and where thieves break in and steal. "But store up for yourselves treasures in*

---

[2] 1 Thessalonians 5:17.

*heaven, where neither moth nor rust destroys, and where thieves do not break in or steal; for where your treasure is, there your heart will be also."*

In this passage, Jesus is challenging the priorities of His listeners. He explains to them that the things people so often consider important, simply aren't. "Where your treasure is, there your heart will be also." It is a very simple fact that we spend our time doing what is important to us. If we say that we love to study God's word, but we don't ever open our Bibles, are we not being dishonest? If we say that we love our families, but we don't spend time with them, are we not being dishonest? If we say we love the Lord, and yet we spend no time with Him, are we not being dishonest? Our hearts are where our treasures are.

When we look back on the past year (or day, for that matter) and consider how we have spent our time, we realize that time spent is an accurate reflection of where our hearts are. That is an uneasy thought. I will never forget one evening as a child, sitting with my family reading the Bible together. I recall being particularly disinterested in reading the Bible that night, and perhaps my father sensed that. He looked up from his Bible, stopped reading, and began to say, "We don't really love the Lord, do we?" My brother and I looked at each other with surprise that such words would ever pass through our father's lips. He was a man very devoted to the Lord, and we could not imagine that he would make such an admission. "We really don't love Him *like we ought* to love Him," he said, "So why don't stop and ask Him to help us *to want* to love Him like we ought." And we prayed. I cannot remember a moment since, that I did not *want to* love the Lord. Of course, my father's words are still as true today as they were then. We do not love Him yet as we ought. But we can walk with Him each moment and learn.

Where is our treasure? Where are our hearts? How can we possibly think about using moments wisely if we haven't fixed our eyes on what is important? I think David understood the importance of treasuring the right things. He said so beautifully in Psalm 19:9-11, "The fear of the LORD is clean, enduring forever; the judgments of the LORD are true; they are righteous altogether. They are more desirable than gold, yes, than much fine gold; sweeter also than honey and the drippings of the honeycomb. Moreover, by them Your servant is warned; in keeping them there is great reward."

# 8

# MENTORING AND REPLICATION:

## A FATHER'S JOY IS NOT BY ACCIDENT

"I have no greater joy than this,
to hear of my children walking in the truth."

With these words from his third letter,[1] John shows us what real fatherhood and mentoring is all about. He underscores the endgame for fathers and mentors. The goal is much simpler than we often consider – that our children walk in the truth. For a father and for anyone who is mentoring another, there is no greater joy.

It is worth noting that John was probably talking about his children in the faith – those he had taught and trained up in Christ. It is encouraging to know that even for those who don't have biological children there is still tremendous opportunity and need for spiritual fathers who will guide and help shape young believers.

In his first letter John gives us a clue about how we can have the great joy of our children walking in the truth. "These things we write, so that our joy may be made complete."[2] These things. *What things?* The things that help us understand the true nature of fellowship (or togetherness) with God and with each other.[3] John wants his readers to

---

[1] 3 John 4.
[2] 1 John 1:3.
[3] 1 John 1:2.

experience in their daily lives the kind of walk with God that Jesus had spoken about in John 17:3, "This is eternal life, that they may know You, the only true God, and Jesus Christ whom You have sent." John adds, "See how great a love the Father has bestowed on us, that we should be called children of God; and such we are…" [4] Our heavenly Father views us as His children – because He has made us that through Christ.

Simply put, John's letters echo what Jesus taught in John 15 – that abiding in Christ will result in fruit and productivity, while not abiding in Him is a total waste. Believers in Jesus have been given eternal life,[5] and that life doesn't begin when we get to heaven; *it begins the moment we believe.* So, we are not waiting for eternal life, we are simply waiting for some of the accompanying joys. Still, we have the opportunity, right here, right now, to walk with Him.

Jesus asks the Father for this very thing: "Sanctify them in the truth; your word is truth…I do not ask on behalf of these alone, but for those also who believe in Me through their word; that they may all be one; even as You, Father, are in Me and I in You…"[6] He prayed for perfect unity among His children, so that "the world may know that You sent Me, and loved them, even as You have loved me."[7] When we are walking with Him, as children, that walk portrays something important about God – something he wants the world to see, *who He is, and what He has done.* Consequently, when we walk in the truth, we walk *with Him.* And when we walk with Him there is joy for us and for Him.[8] That walk doesn't happen by accident, though. Fathers are given the great

---

[4] 1 John 3:1.
[5] John 3:16, John 6:47.
[6] John 17:17, 20-21.
[7] John 17:23.
[8] John 17:13.

responsibility of training up their children in "the discipline and instruction of the Lord."[9]

Fathers – and mentors – if we wish for joy when it comes to our children and those we are leading, then let's follow John's example and invest in our children. Let's lead them by example, teach them to walk in the truth and to walk with Him every moment of every day. Let's show them how to *practice* being with Him: to listen to what He says in His word, to pray without ceasing, and to share His joy with others. What greater gift can a father give his children? And what greater joy can children provide for their father?

---

[9] Ephesians 6:4.

# 9
# SWOT ANALYSIS
## AND PERSONAL GROWTH

SWOT is an acronym for strengths, weaknesses, opportunities, and threats. The analytical tool has been in use for around fifty years, and while some attribute the origin of the SWOT analysis to Stanford Research Institute's Albert Humphrey, because he doesn't take credit for it, the derivation of the device is not clear. Nonetheless, SWOT analysis has been a mainstay of organizational strategy, in part due to its simplicity and exposing power.

The device considers both internal and external factors to help identify areas of improvement and potential areas for emphasis. The SWOT analysis provides a concise snapshot of an organization's present health as well as uncovering opportunities for refinement and growth. The internal factors considered are strengths and weaknesses. Identifying current strengths and weaknesses within the organization helps leaders assess how well the organization is meeting its mission or how badly it is missing the mark. On the external side, opportunities and threats are examined in order to evaluate climate and environment for that organization's function. SWOT analysis is a tool that can help organizations monitor past and present performance (strengths and weaknesses) and to identify action points in anticipation of the future (opportunities and threats).

For example, in the late 1990's Kodak began experiencing significant financial difficulty. Their primary products were film-based. A SWOT analysis for Kodak then would have emphasized that the emerging technologies which were making digital photography much more accessible to the marketplace were a threat to Kodak's film dominance. Little more than a decade later, after being unable to adapt quickly enough, Kodak had to file for Chapter 11 Bankruptcy. Emerging from that process, Kodak has since broadened its product line to account for emerging technologies, and has seen marked financial improvement.

Like most commonsense tools for organizational health and leadership, the SWOT analysis has Biblical parallels, and what can be used to guard and protect organizational health can also be used in self-assessment and personal growth. Let's parse the device one more time, this time to underscore the Biblical principles.

The **internal and past-looking components are the strengths and weaknesses assessment.** The believer in Jesus is told repeatedly to look to the past and present to be aware of strengths and weaknesses. Whereas an organization might compare the strengths and weaknesses to its mission in order to assess the present level of overall success, an individual can do the same. If the highest-order personal goal is to glorify God in all things,[1] then all (intermediate) actions should contribute to the accomplishing of that goal. For example, Christians are told to love one another,[2] and to love everyone else.[3] We are reminded that the one who doesn't love his brother is described as walking around in a blinding darkness.[4]

To assess whether one is strong or weak in love, we can look at the definition of love in 1 Corinthians 13, for example. The chapter first

---

[1] 1 Corinthians 6:20, 10:31.
[2] Romans 12:10, Colossians 3:14.
[3] Romans 13:8.
[4] 1 John 2:11.

describes the centrality of love. If we do great things, but don't have love, we are "nothing."[5] The chapter then describes love in practical terms that make it easy for us to assess:

> Love is patient, love is kind and is not jealous; love does not brag and is not arrogant, does not act unbecomingly; it does not seek its own, is not provoked, does not take into account a wrong suffered, does not rejoice in unrighteousness, but rejoices with the truth; bears all things, believes all things, hopes all things, endures all things. Love never fails.[6]

If I we are not demonstrating these characteristics, then we do not have love – we are not loving. We can assess whether or not love is in our strengths or weaknesses column. And lest we become prideful in identifying love as a strength, we can consider two things: (1) love is not arrogant (pride in being loving is a self-contradictory concept), and (2) love is identified as fruit of the Holy Spirit in the lives of believers[7] thus we can take no credit for our having and showing love. Yet, if we are not showing love, we are worthy of the blame, because we are told to actively walk in submission to the Holy Spirit.[8] Understanding, for example, that the love we have and show will be proportionate to the degree we are submitted to the Holy Spirit,[9] a SWOT analysis of our personal life should draw into sharp focus our relationship with God and how faithfully (or not) we are reflecting that relationship in our daily

---

[5] 1 Corinthians 13:2.
[6] 1 Corinthians 13:4-8a.
[7] Galatians 5:22.
[8] Galatians 5:16.
[9] E.g., Ephesians 5:17-19, Galatians 5:16.

lives. Just as in an organizational assessment, strengths and weaknesses are not identified for purposes of pride, in personal assessment strengths and weaknesses are examined as a status report on faithfulness to the mission (of glorifying Him).

**The external and forward-looking aspects of the SWOT analysis are opportunities and threats.** The threats part is easy: Ephesians 2:1-3 describes three threats to the believer: the world (system, not the people in it), the flesh, and the devil. So the believer must always be on the lookout for how these three things might manifest themselves. The opportunities component can be a bit more challenging, but an honest assessment reveals many opportunities. For example, believers are exhorted in Hebrews 10:24-25 to "consider how to stimulate one another to love and good deeds, not forsaking our own assembling...but encouraging one another..." One opportunity might be to have more committed fellowship with other believers. If we are charged with looking after the well-being of others, and they are charged with looking after ours,[10] then it would only be beneficial to be more engaged with others.

Balanced introspection and self-assessment is a good thing. Obviously an imbalance can be self centered and inappropriate. The SWOT analysis can be a helpful tool to help each one "examine his own work."[11] The principles that are effective for an organization are also effective in one's personal life. And interestingly – though not surprisingly – the basic Biblical principles of faithfulness within an individual's personal life correlate to organizational leadership and health principles. God's word simply works. For those who might be

---

[10] Philippians 2:1-5.
[11] Galatians 6:4.

unknowingly borrowing Biblical principles and seeing their positive fruit, I encourage you to consider the Source, to taste and see that the Lord is good. How blessed is the one who takes refuge in Him.[12]

---

[12] Psalm 34:8.

# 10
# THE TRANSFORMATIVE LEADERSHIP QUOTIENT (TLQ)

## INTRODUCTION

Perhaps the most important aspect of organizational assessment is the assessment of its leadership. Leaders need to be teachable. We need to develop skill in self-assessment and be open to critical assessment from others. The Transformative Leadership Quotient (TLQ) is a metric I am proposing for measuring the quality of a person's ability and equipping to lead in a transformative way, and to assist leaders in better understanding their toolkits and responsibilities as leaders. After finishing this chapter, my hope is that you will be able to use this metric to do your own case studies on various leaders, but most of all to do ongoing self-assessment so that you can be a better leader.

The TLQ focuses not on highlights, but on core qualities of transformative leadership. Transformative learning is focused on an individual's personal growth and personal development – their transformation. This kind of learning is not simply addressing a pedagogy that changes actions or behavior, it is about a kind of learning that enables us to experience real life change. Transformative leadership is the kind of leading that guides others as they walk through the process of transformative learning. Transformative leadership can be expressed at an individual level, it can be engaged at an organizational level, and even at a policy level.

For those who are familiar with the Biblical worldview, this idea will sound very simple. Essentially transformative learning is what Romans 12:1-2 prescribes: being transformed by the renewing of our minds. Transformation by the right kind of learning, or specifically the right content and the right submission to it. According to the apostle Paul, what God has revealed in the Scriptures is that which renews our mind and *that* is what God uses to transform us. Transformative leadership is guiding, helping, leading others through their own process of transformation. If that transformation comes from the application of transformative literature, then the tools for assessing transformative leadership ought to be derived from that very same transformative literature. We have been blessed with a canon of literature that is authoritative (as it claims to be the product of the Creator of all). This text provides us the guidance to make assessments. Of first importance in this discussion is that the TLQ is an attempt to derive a leadership assessment model from the Scriptures themselves.

In leadership assessment models it is very common to recognize the importance of self-awareness, social awareness, self-management, and social management. We will borrow those terms for the TLQ, noting Paul's instructions to Timothy that Timothy guard himself and his teaching.[1] Paul is giving Timothy vital instructions about how to be an outstanding leader within the churches to which Timothy was appointed. Paul cautions him about being attentive to himself first and then attentive to the teaching that he is providing others. That would certainly align with the concept of having awareness of self and being

---

[1] 1 Timothy 4:16.

able to manage oneself well. Timothy was to be self-aware and to manage himself well. He was also to have awareness of others and to be able to manage those interactions with others well. It is worth noting that the Bible offers many leadership principles like these, and many popular leadership principles and management tools are derived straight from the word of the greatest Leader of all, the One who created humanity and understands how we grow and develop. In this context we are trying to extract the principles He provides. Here we discover the importance to leadership of the principles of self-awareness, social awareness, self-management, and social management.

Self-awareness involves a recognition of who one is, what tools and skills one has, and what one needs in order to refine and grow. Social awareness involves the same three components facing outward: a recognition of who others are, of what their skills are, and what their needs are. Self-management is the designed engagement in growth and the proper self-expression in the various stewardships we have including in service to others. Social management is the designed engagement in pursuing the growth of others and their own proper self-expression. These four characteristics seem an appropriate grouping with which to begin our evaluation.

Based on the canon of transformative literature,[2] we discover an emphasis on four persons who exemplify in different ways these four characteristics. Of course, we begin with Jesus, who is the perfect example, as the God-man. We also recognize the leadership acumen of Paul, Nehemiah, and Moses. The Scriptures provide significant data about each, showing them to be exemplary leaders, exhibiting vital core

---

[2] By which I mean the Hebrew Scriptures and the Greek New Testament, or what we commonly refer to as the *Bible*.

leadership characteristics. While there are certainly other key leaders identified in Scripture – perhaps most notably David and Peter – we will focus on these four, simply due to the Scriptural data covering their leadership tools and roles. Before we begin examining these four leaders, we need to acknowledge that such an analysis has inherent limitations.

First, the leadership data at our disposal is descriptive rather than prescriptive. It describes the four characters and what they did. We are extracting principles from their character and actions. We need, then, to exercise great caution in drawing prescriptions from descriptive material (historical narrative in the Scriptures). Second, it is fair to critique this approach as somewhat subjective. Who determines which characteristics are most important and which ones should be most emphasized? While I have sought to draw out the characteristics and actions of these men carefully and objectively, I recognize that my perspective is not omniscient, and that my descriptions here are somewhat subjective. Of course, that limitation is inherent in any human application of any principles. Still, I want to be transparent and acknowledge that limitation. Finally, I also recognize that I am providing a qualitative basis for a quantitative quotient. The metric is rooted in qualitative rather than quantitative data. In short, the TLQ has limitations, but I anticipate that it is effective enough, as it keeps us focused on the Author and Perfector of the faith which provides us transformation in the first place.[3] Further it draws our gaze to praiseworthy things and encourages us to dwell on these things.[4] While the TLQ has limitations, it is worthwhile because of the source of the

---

[3] Hebrews 12:1.
[4] Philippians 4:8.

data (Scripture) and the subjects who we are seeking to emulate (Jesus in particular, along with Paul, Nehemiah, and Moses).

## EXEMPLARY LEADERSHIP
## OF JESUS, PAUL, NEHEMIAH, AND MOSES

While we could write volumes about the leadership traits Jesus demonstrated during His ministry on earth, we want to narrow the focus to five aspects. First, we are told to think like Jesus with respect to His willingness to sacrifice Himself for the well-being of others.[5] He was equal with God, sharing His Father's glory, yet He humbled Himself to the point of becoming a man and dying the death of a common criminal – the excruciating death of crucifixion. In this Jesus demonstrates incredible **self-sacrifice** and **humility**. We also find Jesus expending a great deal of time and energy **investing in people**.[6] For several years He spent much of His days pouring into His disciples, preparing them for the tasks He had for them. He is deliberate in His teaching, as He often provides **communication of the big picture and the details**[7] for His disciples. Jesus is also very direct in His explanation and promotion of proper **priorities**.[8]

The apostle Paul, appointed and commissioned by Jesus, was a mentor and leader whose approach was characterized by **prayer for those he was serving**.[9] We read on numerous occasions of how his love for people drove him to pray for them, especially for their growth

---

[5] Philippians 2:1-11.
[6] Matthew 13ff, and John 13-17.
[7] E.g., Matthew 24, and John 13-17.
[8] John 12:23-26.
[9] Ephesians 1:14ff, 3:14ff, Philippians 1:8-11.

and spiritual wellbeing. He was **driven and focused**,[10] dedicating his life to do everything possible in the fulfillment of his stewardships. He counted everything as worthless in comparison to his relationship with God and the tasks God had given him. Paul wasn't selfish about those endeavors. He was deeply **passionate about people's success.**[11] He rejoiced in the growth of the Thessalonians, treating them as if he was a loving mother to them. Paul **instilled *true* culture;**[12] he didn't lead people astray. Rather, he was diligent to ensure that those he was serving knew the truth, were well trained, and were prepared for the challenges ahead. As he directed Timothy and Titus, Paul also provided a list of **general leadership qualifications** – of the traits to look for in church leadership candidates.[13]

Nehemiah, the fifth-century BC post-exilic leader in Israel was extraordinary. On more than one occasion he risked his life to serve and lead well. When he was faced with severe problems, he was **prayerful** about how he could make a difference.[14] When he saw the plight of the city of Jerusalem, he prayed and expressed a willingness to be personally involved. He was **courageous** to bring the problem to King Artaxerxes, though it could have resulted in Nehemiah's death.[15] He didn't make decisions lightly, demonstrating a **commitment to assessment** as he personally inspected the walls of Jerusalem before determining his strategy.[16] Nehemiah **worked with people**.[17] He didn't delegate and

---

[10] Philippians 2:3b-9.
[11] 1 Thessalonians 3:6-10, Philippians 1:3-6.
[12] Acts 20:26-28, 2 Timothy 2:2.
[13] 1 Timothy 3, Titus 1.
[14] Nehemiah 1:5-11, 4:9.
[15] Nehemiah 2:1 and 4:4-6.
[16] Nehemiah 2:15.
[17] Nehemiah 4:15-23.

watch from afar, he did himself what he asked others to do. He was a **unifier**,[18] wisely discerning difficulties and judging between brothers. He wasn't focused on personal gain. He **served first** and considered personal benefit as an afterthought.[19] He didn't stop until the task was completed. Nehemiah was a **finisher**.[20] Throughout his tenure he was **mission focused**,[21] engaging the task at hand until the job was done and the walls of Jerusalem were completed. Even after that task was completed, Nehemiah served as governor and led well.

Moses provides perhaps the earliest and most comprehensive example of a leader, as we read in the Torah of his commissioning by God and his days leading Israel as God's representative. Moses was given extraordinary gifts and opportunities, but he did not grow proud, nor did he exert his own will. He had a keen **awareness of the Source of his empowerment**.[22] On numerous occasions we encounter Moses **speaking candidly with God**.[23] While Moses looked forward to God's promise fulfillment, Moses demonstrated a **respect for the past**.[24] He took seriously the commitment made long in the past regarding Joseph's remains being carried out of Egypt, and he was quick to memorialize the works of God. Moses was appointed to lead Israel, but he **viewed himself as a servant of God** (Exodus 14:31). He was tirelessly willing to be **available to the people** he was leading.[25] When that task became

---

[18] Nehemiah 5:1-13.
[19] Nehemiah 5:16-19.
[20] Nehemiah 6:15.
[21] Nehemiah 5:14-19.
[22] Exodus 4:10-13.
[23] E.g., Exodus 5:22-23.
[24] Exodus 13:19, Exodus 15.
[25] Exodus 18:13.

too great for one person, Moses received counsel and **adopted a systematic model for delegation.**[26]

## QUANTIFYING CORE LEADERSHIP CHARACTERISTICS

**Step #1: Extracting the Traits**

The traits, character, and leadership tools exhibited by Jesus and also by Paul, Nehemiah, and Moses underscore the depth of quality needed to lead well. To extract the essence of leadership evident in Scripture, we consider a composite of each of the traits highlighted above. Together these twelve traits comprise the TLQ's core characteristics of high-quality leadership. In no particular order, these are:

> Humility and Self Sacrifice
> Concern for the Well-being and Growth of Others
> Investment in Others
> Working with Others
> Communication and Instillation of Truth
> Assessment and Accountability
> Prioritization, Organization, and Mission Commitment
> Drive and Finish
> Prayerfulness
> Courage
> Unifying
> Contextual Awareness

---

[26] Exodus 18:13-26.

**Step #2: Establishing a Scale**

In order to devise a quantification from these qualitative traits, we rank these leadership characteristics based on the sheer relative volume of data regarding the specific leadership activities of each individual. To the characteristics observed in Jesus's ministry, we assign a value of 4. To those of Paul, 3. To Nehemiah's, 2. Finally, to the traits of Moses, a value of 1. One might argue that due to the volume of Moses's writings and the length of his ministry, that Moses's leadership is more prominent. Perhaps this is so, however, based on the *relative* volume of material we will rank Nehemiah's a bit higher. Nehemiah's writing is arguably more densely filled with leadership material, while Moses's writing covers a much broader scope and focuses less on leadership aspects. Of course, some might argue in favor of flipping the rankings of Moses's traits over Nehemiah's, but for purposes of this beta test, Nehemiah's leadership density wins out. Further, as Jesus is the perfect leader, we can demonstrate that He showed every single one of these traits, and we will apply His ranking to each one.

Jesus and Paul poured into individuals, while Nehemiah and Moses served the people in general. Jesus and Paul get points for the personal investment in others. Nehemiah earns points for actually working at physical labor, hand in hand with others. While Nehemiah and Moses were both committed to God's truth, Paul especially gave intense personal effort to communicating and instilling God's truth. While Jesus, Paul, and Nehemiah deal directly with assessment and accountability, Moses seemed a bit less deliberate in that regard. Moses didn't finish quite as well as the others, so he did not receive a ranking on that trait. All demonstrated remarkable courage, but Moses had some lapses. Nehemiah was especially focused on unifying the people, while Paul and Moses exhorted the people in that regard, but perhaps weren't as personally involved as was Nehemiah to ensure practical unity. All seemed to have strong contextual awareness, though there seems no evidence that Nehemiah understood the prophetic weight of his endeavor. Of course, these are subjective assessments, and debatable ones at that. Nonetheless, based on the passages considered and the rationale described, the characteristics and their assigned points are as follows:

> Humility and Self Sacrifice 4321
> Concern for the Well-being and Growth of Others 4321
> Investment in Others 43
> Working with Others 42
> Communication and Instillation of Truth 43
> Assessment and Accountability 432
> Prioritization, Organization, and Mission Commitment 4321
> Drive and Finish 432
> Prayerfulness 4321
> Courage 432
> Unifying 42
> Contextual Awareness 431

**Step #3: Organizing the Traits**

Next, we add the point totals and divide the qualities between those pertaining to self and those pertaining to social.

Pertaining to Self-Awareness and Management
> Humility and Self Sacrifice 10
> Prayerfulness 10
> Prioritization, Organization, and Mission Commitment 10

Concern for the Wellbeing and Growth of Others 10
Courage 9
Assessment and Accountability 9
Drive and Finish 9
Total: 67 Points
Pertaining to Social Awareness and Management
Contextual Awareness 8
Investment in Others 7
Communication and Instillation of Truth 7
Working with Others 6
Unifying 6
Total: 34 Points

Composite Total: 101 Points

## THE TRANSFORMATIVE LEADERSHIP QUOTIENT (TLQ)

Now that we have extracted the traits from the data source, established a scale, and organized and quantified the traits, we formalize the instrument to arrive at a TLQ. The instrument is a two-part survey. The first section is a self-assessment of how strongly the subject agrees they possess all twelve traits. The second is a peer assessment of the subject on how strongly the peer agrees that the subject possesses all twelve traits. The instrument utilizes the Likert 5-point scale, and answers will be scored as follows:

Strongly Agree – 5
Agree – 4
Not Sure – 3

Disagree – 2
Strongly Disagree – 1

The self-assessment answers all twelve traits with the level of agreement points (1-5) per answer, multiplied by the number of points assigned to that trait. (For example, a "strongly agree" on humility and self-sacrifice would net 50 points, while a strongly agree on drive and finish would net 45 points.) The total number of self-assessment points are multiplied by .67 to arrive at the self-assessment score, because the self-awareness and management traits total 67 points. The formula for this is:

$$\text{Total Points} \times .67 = \text{SA}$$

The peer-assessment also answers all twelve traits, likewise, with the level of agreement points. The total number of peer assessment points are multiplied by .34, as the social awareness and management traits total 34 points. The formula for this is:

$$\text{Total Points} \times .34 = \text{PA}$$

The two scores averaged equals the TLQ. The final formula to calculate the TLQ is:

$$\text{SA} + \text{PA} \div 2 = \text{TLQ}$$

# THE TLQ INSTRUMENT

Using the following scale, answer for each of the 12 traits how strongly you agree that you demonstrate the respective leadership trait:

Strongly Agree – 5
Agree – 4
Not Sure – 3
Disagree – 2
Strongly Disagree – 1

## Section 1: Pertaining to Self-Awareness and Management

Humility and Self Sacrifice                    Points X 10 _____
Prayerfulness                                        Points X 10 _____
Prioritization, Organization, and Mission Commitment
                                                            Points X 10 _____
Concern for the Wellbeing and Growth of Others
                                                            Points X 10 _____
Courage                                              Points X 9 _____
Assessment and Accountability             Points X 9 _____
Drive and Finish                                    Points X 9 _____

Total: 67 Points     (Possible 335)          Total Section Points _____

## Section 2: Pertaining to Social Awareness and Management

Contextual Awareness                          Points X 8 _____
Investment in Others                            Points X 7 _____
Communication and Instillation of Truth   Points X 7 _____
Working with Others                            Points X 6 _____
Unifying                                              Points X 6 _____

Total: 34 Points (Possible 170)              Total Section Points _____

(SA) Self-Assessment Composite Total: 101 Points (Possible 505)
                                                  Total Points X .67 =_____
(PA) Peer Assessment Composite Total: 101 Points (Possible 505)
                                                  Total Points X .34 =_____

$$SA + PA \div 2 = TLQ \underline{\hspace{3cm}}$$

CONCLUSION

While the TLQ has obvious subjective elements, the instrument offers a quantitative tool for assessing transformative leadership qualities and preparedness once the (subjective) baseline is established. The tool can be used to compare a leader's own perceived readiness with peers' perceptions of the leader's perceived readiness. More importantly the TLQ can help the leader to evaluate with reference to Biblical standards for leadership quality. Even if it does not provide a fully objective metric, the analytical and comparative processes offer a useful exercise in self and peer assessment. Further, the TLQ can be adapted to utilize the leadership acumen of other Biblical leaders (David and Peter, for example) in order to provide a more comprehensive glimpse at Biblical expectations for leaders.

# ORGANIZATIONAL LEADERSHIP

# 11
# ORGANIZATIONAL LEADERSHIP:
## INVESTING IN SHARED PURPOSE

### AWARENESS AND COMMUNICATION
### OF THE DESTINATION AND THE PATH

One question I often challenge individuals and organizations with is this: "If in five years, your enterprise or initiative fails, what went wrong?" What I am challenging them to think about is what are the intermediate and short-term threats and potential for failure that might lead to an overall failure. From the perspective of looking back from a not yet realized outcome, what were the factors that contributed to failure? It is helpful to look forward, look backward, and then reassess what needs to be done now.

It works the same way with success: There are many small steps along the path to a positive outcome, and every one of those small steps is just as important to the process as the outcome. So while it is important to look forward to the outcome, we have to be diligently focused on the intermediate steps and details. Think of how compounding interest works – the first year's tiny gains are just as important as the last year's huge gains, even if the amounts are drastically different. Ultimately, turning our eyes on Jesus is the way we can endure toward the right outcome,[1] but there are specific expressions of that

---

[1] Hebrews 12:1-3.

focus we have to keep in mind as we go, such as abiding in Him,[2] letting His word dwell richly in us,[3] walking in His Spirit,[4] etc.

In order to help people see what they need to see so they can fulfill their roles and ministries, they have to be able to recognize the potential outcomes – they need to see the same destination and the path you do. That requires a great deal of listening and observation on the part of the leader, and a willingness to understand where people are and how the leader can interact with their context. As a leader listens and observes, he or she can communicate in a relatable and approachable way where the group is headed, how they are going to get there, and how each person plays a vital role. In the body of Christ there are many members, but one body.[5] Each person has a role, and leadership must recognize the uniqueness and individuality of those fulfilling each role, and understand (by listening and observing) how to best communicate with each one. It really boils down to loving the people you are leading. The same applies in any leadership context.

## PASSION, PURPOSE, AND PLANNING

Personally, I am impassioned and optimistic because of four things: (1) the transcendent purpose (the opportunity to glorify God by fulfilling a mission), (2) the divine enablement (God's provision for the task at hand – He gave us the task, and we can trust Him to strengthen us for it), (3) commitment to being prepared (diligence in developing what He has provided can make the difference between being ready

---

[2] John 15.
[3] Colossians 3.
[4] Galatians 5.
[5] 1 Corinthians 12:12.

when He opens a door, or failing to seize an opportunity when He makes it available), and (4) camaraderie in labor. We don't labor alone. The Christian life – and every enterprise in it – is a team sport. We need to value and invest in people and love and support them as we encourage them to meet His design for them. **Ultimately, leadership is investing in people to help them fulfill what God has designed from them to be and do.** Hebrews 10:24 challenges us to consider ways to motivate and encourage one another to love and good deeds.

The ultimate shared purpose is in worshipping Him as worthy of glory through the enterprise of expressing His love to people. It's about serving with Him, serving Him, and serving Him with others. Whatever the enterprise is – producing or selling widgets – it all should be done for His glory[6] and in His name.[7] This means that the organizational cause offers significance and meaning, because of *who* the organization is about and its *purpose* in serving. Too often we mistake *plans* for the *cause* (means with the end). But the great cause for one who knows Christ is wrapped up in knowing and honoring God. The *plans* are the intermediate steps to fulfilling that.

The cause is not negotiable. Plans must be. This is where people see authentic commitment to mission, and where they also see flexibility, consideration, and understanding in how to get there. Firm and flexible are not mutually exclusive leadership traits. In one context Paul described his leadership and service as gentle and caring,[8] ultimately for the benefit of those he was leading. Paul includes both elements of "speaking the truth in love."[9] If the communication is true, it will be

---

[6] 1 Corinthians 10:31.
[7] Colossians 3:17.
[8] 1 Thessalonians 2:7.
[9] Ephesians 4:15.

authentic, and usually received as authentic. That in itself is inspirational. But if the communication is *also* in love, that allows authenticity to become personal. When people know that a leader truly cares for them and is looking out for their best interests, that is where the seeds of loyalty sprout and bear fruit. Because leaders have such power through this dynamic, it is vital that they are truthful and loving, and not simply using these two concepts to be manipulative. It has been said that there are two ways to effect behavior in others: to manipulate or to inspire. So much emotionally charged communication can be intended for control or manipulation. It is much better to inspire people by simply being the right kind of person to those they are leading. People follow inspiring leadership, and are blessed when leaders are seeking the good of those they are leading.

# 12
# THE VERITAS FORMULA
## FOR ORGANIZATIONAL LEADERSHIP

The VERITAS formula for organizational leadership is really about leading people and helping them to become who they are designed to be. The formula is rooted in the principle that from God's mouth comes knowledge and understanding.[1] God's word is true, and is thus reliable as the undergirding for life. The Scriptures have much to say about leading people, and seven Biblical principles make up the VERITAS formula.

## VOICE
### (PROVERBS 1:5)

*"A wise man will hear and increase in learning, and a man of understanding will acquire wise counsel."*

The leader who acknowledges the voice of others demonstrates that people are valued, that they can contribute, and even that their contribution is needed. Being allowed to have a voice humanizes a person in a way for which they were designed. God created humanity in His image, and He expresses His own voice. To deprive a person of their voice deprives them of an important expression of who they were created to be.

---

[1] Proverbs 2:6.

**In practice**, leaders are encouraged to ensure that the organizational culture fosters and promotes candid communication and transparency. It is important that there be opportunities and outlets for people to use their voice – to have an influential say in the organization. Ultimately, leaders who listen to the people in their organizations will have a much more accurate perspective of the organization itself. **In personal growth**, the voice of others should be part of the wise counsel that keeps leaders humble, teachable, and connected.

## EMPOWERMENT
### (1 CORINTHIANS 9:24)

*"Do you not know that those who run in a race all run, but only one receives the prize? Run in such a way that you may win."*

After describing his ultimate prize,[2] Paul encourages his readers to run as if to win. In his letter Paul also provides his readers the tools they need in order to be able to run properly. If we are expected to run as if to win, we must put those with whom we are entrusted in position to run as well. Leaders should be focused on empowering people to fulfill their roles. If we are called to run as if in a race, then in order to meet that challenge, leaders should be focused on providing the tools, the opportunities, and even the freedom to be able to run well. For example, the writer of Hebrews encourages his readers to "run with endurance the race set before us, fixing our eyes on Jesus..."[3] A wise leader will create an environment that encourages people to implement

---

[2] 1 Corinthians 9:23.
[3] Hebrews 12:1b-2a.

the tools provided to run the race. As Eric Liddell said in *Chariots of Fire*, "I believe God made me for a purpose, but he also made me fast. And when I run I feel His pleasure."[4] Allow people who are serving with you to feel God's pleasure.

**In practice**, remove the shackles from people, guard against the shackles' return, and allow people to run. Sometimes they will stumble, sometimes they will fall. Be there to cushion the blow and help them get back up. **In personal growth**, it is vital that leaders allow people the room to refine methods and processes. In short: avoid micromanaging.

## RESPONSIBILITY
### (PHILIPPIANS 1:5-6, 1 CORINTHIANS 15:58)

*"...in view of your participation in the gospel from the first day until now. For I am confident of this very thing, that He who began a good work in you will complete it until the day of Christ Jesus."*

*"Therefore, my beloved brethren, be steadfast, immovable, always abounding in the work of the Lord, knowing that your toil is not in vain in the Lord."*

The Philippians had embraced the responsibility of investing in the gospel, and there was to be an outcome. Paul was confident that God would ultimately bring the work to fruition. Their work was not insignificant, and it was not without implications. Paul thought it important to communicate to the Philippians the significance of their work and to encourage them about the progress of that work. Likewise,

---

[4] Colin Welland and Hugh Hudson, *Chariots of Fire*, Twentieth Century Fox Film Corporation, 1981.

leaders need to help the people they are leading understand the significance of their own work and show them what the results of their labor might be. Similarly, Paul reminded the Corinthians that their work had value because of Who their work was for. Solomon contrasts this by saying that all is vanity and there is no advantage in "under the sun" work (Ecc 1:2-3). There is something that makes work significant, and leaders ought to recognize what that is, looking beyond the sun for that significance.

**In practice**, leaders should realize that when people understand the big picture, and can see a transcendent reason for their work, they will embrace the responsibility of their labor. **In personal growth**, it is important not to be so focused on outcomes that we become oblivious to the value of the action itself, however if we are working toward the right goals it is helpful to focus on the big picture.

## INDEPENDENCE
### (1 CORINTHIANS 12:7, 1 PETER 4:10)

*"But to each one is given the manifestation of the Spirit for the common good."*

*"As each one has received a special gift, employ it in serving one another as good stewards of the manifold grace of God."*

Paul encourages the Corinthians that every believer is given a manifestation or outworking of the Holy Spirit. Each one is responsible to utilize what the Spirit gives them, and needs to understand their individual capability and responsibility in doing so. Likewise, Peter encourages his readers, as individuals, to employ their special gifts. It is notable that in both of these contexts the giftings are to be used for the benefit of others; still they are individual functions.

**In practice,** wise leaders understand that people need the latitude to function as independently as possible, yet always with a view toward benefiting others through those functions. There is a certain degree of independence needed, while not losing sight of the intended beneficiaries. Let people think for themselves, using their skills to the utmost, and help them see how their personal excellence contributes to the good of those with whom they work.

**In personal growth,** leaders should learn all they can about the functions assigned to people, in order to understand what causes limitations and what overcomes those limitations. The goal of the leader in this context is to foster maturity and independence of individuals within the effective function of the organization. Individuals matter. God uses individuals to accomplish His task, which is the growth and maturing of the body of Christ (the church). We must recognize the power of the individual and harness it appropriately for the growth and benefit of the team.

## TEAMWORK
### (EPHESIANS 4:31-32, HEBREWS 10:24-25A)

*"Let all bitterness and wrath and anger and clamor and slander be put away from you, along with all malice. Be kind to one another, tender-hearted, forgiving each other, just as God in Christ also has forgiven you."*

*"and let us consider how to stimulate one another to love and good deeds, not forsaking our own assembling together…"*

The previous two passages[5] both emphasize the importance of the individual while insisting on the importance of their contributions to others. Independent function is vital but is designed for the purpose of benefitting others. In light of this, Paul encourages his readers that they need to treat each other appropriately – as God has treated them. There is no room for leaders or followers to be unkind, wrathful, or unforgiving. Leaders especially should be modeling kindness, gentleness, forgiveness, etc. Those following will be responsive to that kind of leadership.

Further, the writer of Hebrews challenges his readers to constantly be considering how to encourage each other to love and good deeds. It is especially interesting to note that these two components are the necessary core of any positive business ethics atmosphere. Good deeds stem from and are identified by the core values – *what is truly loved by leadership*. It is true that where one's heart is the feet will follow. If our love is targeted correctly, then we will have a reliable matrix for understanding what is *good*. If not, then good gets fuzzy. Leaders need to understand what (or who) is worthy of love and why. Only then can we encourage others to do *good*. This is the fundamental core of any quality team.

Another vital element embedded in the Hebrews passage is the importance of assembling together. One cannot benefit others if that person is not (at least occasionally) actually *with* others. Wise leaders will foster fellowship and camaraderie, helping people to see and understand the people whom they are serving.

**In practice**, while leaders must caution against causing death of a thousand meetings, it is vital that we understand the importance of

---

[5] 1 Corinthians 12:7 and 1 Peter 4:10.

bringing people together to listen, to learn, to serve, and to grow. Leaders must also demonstrate, communicate, and instill core values. In observing this, individual members of the team will understand what the team is all about, and how to benefit the team.

**In personal growth**, leaders must first *be* before we can *do*. Telling others to be gentle, kind, and forgiving is of little value unless leaders first demonstrates that fruit. Further, where one's heart is there his treasure will be.[6] If one's core values are not in the right place, it will eventually become apparent to all.

## ACCOUNTABILITY
## (1 CORINTHIANS 12:12, EPHESIANS 5:21)

*"For even as the body is one and yet has many members, and all the members of the body, though they are many, are one body, so also is Christ."*

*"Subject yourselves to one another in the fear of Christ."*

*"Have this thinking in you that was also in Christ Jesus…"*

People are to be capable and empowered to function independently, yet not as separated from the group, and not simply for one's own personal gain, but for the benefit of others. In the body of Christ there are many individual members, yet they are all equally valuable members of one body. As such, they are reminded to have the same kind of humility as Christ did – He humbled Himself even to the point of death on a cross for the benefit of all. If the Creator of all was

---

[6] Matthew 6:21.

willing to become like one of His creations and suffer and die on their behalf (so that by believing in Him they might have true life), then how can we be unwilling to show the same humility? Further, if we have that humility, then we should regard each other as more worthy of honor than ourselves,[7] and we should be willing to subject to each other.

**In practice**, leaders must recognize that we are not above those we are leading. Like Christ, we must be willing to bring ourselves low for the benefit of others. If a leader is unwilling to do this, their ability to lead is hampered, and they will only be able to develop people to a small extent. However, if leaders are willing to be transparent and accountable to those whom we are leading – those leaders have the capacity to help people excel at the highest levels. *This* is inspirational leadership. Leaders who will lead by example and do even the most menial of tasks are the most respected and the most influential leaders. *These* are the kinds of leaders who are beloved and not simply followed.

**In personal growth**, it is hard for any leader to try to emulate the thinking and character of the greatest Leader unless we have a personal relationship with Him. If a leader doesn't know Christ, we can borrow concepts from His worldview and understand that His principles work, and we can be effective, influential, and even beloved leaders. But we cannot reach the heights for which we were intended unless we have received the blessing that Christ humbled Himself to provide for us. Taste and see that the Lord is good. How blessed is the one who takes refuge in Him.[8] Jesus adds that, "I am the vine, you are the branches; he who abides in Me and I in him, he bears much fruit, for apart from Me you can do nothing."[9]

---

[7] Philippians 2:3.

[8] Psalm 34:8.

[9] John 15:5.

## SUPPORT
## (GALATIANS 6:2, 6:10, HEBREWS 10:24)

*"Bear one another's burdens, and thereby fulfill the law of Christ."*

*"So then, while we have opportunity, let us do good to all people, and especially to those who are of the household of the faith."*

*"and let us consider how to stimulate one another to love and good deeds..."*

The law of Christ is love.[10] One significant expression of that love is to bear one another's burdens. When one struggles, all struggle. When one weeps, all weep.[11] In a leadership context, leaders ought to consider the burdens of those working with them as belonging not just to those working, but to the leaders themselves. Expressing love in that setting requires that leaders provide the same support and resources they would want for themselves to deal with whatever the burden might be. If leaders aren't properly supporting those whom they are leading, they are not expressing the requisite love of Christ, and if they are not doing that, they simply are not good leaders.

Paul adds another important nuance in Galatians 6:10 – doing good should start at home – as he describes it, in the household of faith. Paul is encouraging Christians to *first* do good to other Christians and *then* to do good to all humanity. It is not a matter of *either or*, it is a *both and*, but with a stated priority: doing good starts at home.

---

[10] Matthew 22:37-40, John 13:34.
[11] Romans 12:15.

In a leadership context sometimes we get this wrong. We can focus so much on the customer or consumer who is purchasing the product or service we are providing, that we forget that the organization itself – the leaders and those whom they are leading – constitute a household of sorts. Take care of those at home, and they will be able to take care of others.

**In practice**, this means to prioritize the support and care of those being led over the support and care for those outside the organization. Consequently, the customer is not always right. There are scenarios in which meeting a customer's demand is not the right thing to do. Guard the dignity of those serving with you, and support them in every way you can. A fringe benefit of doing the right thing in properly supporting those serving with you is that they will blossom in their roles and will be able to provide the highest quality products and services.

**In personal growth**, this means constantly considering ways to stimulate and encourage personal growth in others.[12] It demands a focus on the wellbeing of others, and a commitment to actually doing the things needed for their development.

## CONCLUSION

In short, the VERITAS formula for organizational leadership is a Biblical formula for demonstrating Christlike love to others. It is far more focused on people than on products and outcomes, and yet, remarkably, it always produces excellent outcomes. This pattern seems consistent with the teachings of Christ. In a moment of counterintuitive (to us, perhaps) teaching, Christ said, "He who loves his life loses it, and

---

[12] Hebrews 10:24.

he who hates his life in this world will keep it to life eternal."[13] He was challenging His listeners to realign their priorities to reflect a total focus on Him. In so doing He highlighted the principle that following His patterns always leads to the best outcomes, even if in the short term the cost seems too high. And so it is with leadership. Following His model is always the best path.

Even those who choose to reject Him as their Sovereign will often affirm His wisdom unknowingly as they borrow His principles and apply them to their own lives. They see positive results and pat themselves on the back for being so skilled in leadership. Sadly, this is like receiving a precious gift and never acknowledging the Giver. So I simply urge leaders who apply these principles and discover how effective they can be, to give credit to the One to Whom all credit is due. From the mouth of God comes knowledge and understanding![14]

---

[13] John 12:25.
[14] Proverbs 2:6.

# 13
# AVOIDING
# MISSION DRIFT
## A CASE STUDY FROM EPHESUS

## INTRODUCTION

The demise of the church at Ephesus illustrates how difficult it is to safeguard the worldview core of an institution. The church there had every advantage, including the personal ministries of Paul and Timothy. Yet, within thirty years that church had abandoned the first principles of their worldview: the church left its first love. As educational leaders we need to be aware of how rapidly and why worldview drift can take place. Here we examine the Ephesus model and demise in order to uncover steps that we as educational leaders can take to safeguard the mission and worldview core of the institutions with which we have been entrusted. First we need to understand the problem.

## UNDERSTANDING THE PROBLEM

Friedrich Nietzsche once famously said that God was dead, and that we have killed Him.[1] In his story Nietzsche was communicating that we have created a narrative using tools of science and discovery, and in that narrative God is simply no longer necessary. Nietzsche described

---

[1] Friedrich Nietzsche, *The Gay Science* (1882, 1887) para. 125; Walter Kaufmann ed. (New York: Vintage, 1974), 181-82.

churches as the sepulchers – the graves of God. He viewed the churches as the last place where God was memorialized – God's final resting place. From that perspective, involvement in faith-based activity would be little more than a celebration of the irrelevant, the impotent, and the failed past.

Similarly, Christopher Hitchens mused that religion was simply humanity's first crack at trying to figure things out, and once we advance past those embarrassingly ignorant conclusions we can move on to things that actually have some connection to reality.[2] Bill Nye warned against Christianity on economic grounds. He asked how we could expect to excel economically if we as a country continued to educate our children in anti-scientific myths – like the one that recounts how God created the world in six days.[3] Others have questioned not only the wisdom of a Biblical worldview, but even the sanity of it. Bill Maher, for example, has mocked that Christianity – and belief systems like it– are symptoms of mental illness.[4]

This is the society in which we now live – appropriately described by some as *post-Christian*. As we have applied Nietzsche's declaration of independence from God, we grow increasingly uncomfortable with the things of God. This generation largely views the things of God as inconsequential at best and sinister at worst.

These secular conclusions have had dramatic impact on the perceived relevance of faith expression in general, and according to the Barna Group, among those aged thirty and under in America, only

---

[2] Christopher Hitchens, *The Portable Atheist: Essential Readings for the Nonbeliever* (Philadelphia, PA: DaCapo Press, 2007), xvii.
[3] Bill Nye, *Undeniable: Evolution and the Science of Creation* (New York, NY: St. Martins Press, 2014), 11-21.
[4] http://www.celebatheists.com/wiki/Bill_Maher.

twenty percent believe church attendance is important, compared with forty-nine percent of all adults who still believe that church is at least somewhat valuable.[5] The trajectory – especially among younger people – is sharply secular. This climate is especially uncomfortable for leaders of Christian institutions who face the daily tug of war between increasing the constituency and maintaining core Biblical values. When the culture and the dollars are running away from Christianity, how can leaders of Christian institutions maintain a Biblical focus without financially ruining the schools over which they preside?

In 2013, Valley Forge Christian College was ranked by Forbes as having the second worst return on investment for students. Commenting on that ranking, Forbes' Susan Adams observed that, "Not surprisingly for a Christian school, students tend to earn degrees in religious studies, which don't lead to the most lucrative careers."[6] Valley Forge Christian College's strategy (in part to overcome that reputation) was to move toward a university model, changing their name to Valley Forge University. Valley Forge's President, Dr. Don Meyer explained why the name Valley Forge University was chosen over Valley Forge Christian University: "Other names were discussed including Valley Forge Christian University. Unfortunately, the name Christian is not welcomed in some places in the world and even now, we have some alumni requesting their degrees without that name."[7]

---

[5] The Barna Group, "Americans Divided on the Importance of Church" at https://www.barna.org/barna-update/culture/661-americans-divided-on-the-importance-of-church#.Vi8Xoq6rTeR.

[6] Susan Adams, "The 25 Colleges With the Worst Return on Investment," Forbes, at http://www.forbes.com/sites/susanadams/2013/08/09/the-25-colleges-with-the-worst-return-on-investment/.

[7] "New Name, Same Mission" at http://www.valleyforge.edu/about/new-name-same-mission.

Valley Forge is not an exceptional case. More and more Christian institutions are moving to the university model with neutral labeling, in order to help shore up the return on investment deficiency. Accredited education is very expensive, and as Susan Adams recognized, expensive Christian educations don't typically provide requisite financial returns. Shrewd leaders are recognizing that they have to deal with this challenge head on, that increased financial pressures make it more and more difficult to retain core values. Now, this is not intended as a critique of the university model nor of neutral branding – in fact, those moves can be very helpful, and are advisable in many cases. But these moves do illustrate the very real pressure to advance beyond traditional operations in order to sustain financial viability, and accompanying that pressure are increased opportunities for worldview drift.

So the question remains an important one: What strategies can leaders of Christian institutions employ in order to ensure that, even as they seek to wisely adapt to the needs of the day, they keep their institutions steadily grounded in a Biblical worldview? To answer the question, we turn to the first-century church at Ephesus, to consider the early lifecycle of that church and the roots of its demise, and to extract some important principles for how leaders can help guard their institutions from worldview drift.

## A CASE STUDY: THE CHURCH AT EPHESUS

We are first introduced to the city of Ephesus in Acts 18, where Paul entered the synagogue and reasoned with the Jews:

They came to Ephesus, and he left them there. Now he himself entered the synagogue and reasoned with the Jews.[8]

On a later visit to Ephesus, Paul found some disciples there.

It happened that while Apollos was at Corinth, Paul passed through the upper country and came to Ephesus, and found some disciples.[9]

In addition to teaching them, he made a practice of entering the synagogue for three months, where he proclaimed, reasoned, and persuaded regarding the kingdom of God.

And he entered the synagogue and continued speaking out boldly for three months, reasoning and persuading *them* about the kingdom of God.[10]

Some responded very harshly, causing Paul to move away from the synagogue with those who became disciples, taking up reasoning with them at the school of Tyrannus[11] for a duration of two years.[12]

But when some were becoming hardened and disobedient, speaking evil of the Way before the people, he withdrew from them and took away the disciples, reasoning daily in the school

---

[8] Acts 18:19.
[9] Acts 19:1.
[10] Acts 19:8.
[11] Acts 19:9.
[12] Acts 19:10.

of Tyrannus. This took place for two years, so that all who lived in Asia heard the word of the Lord, both Jews and Greeks.[13]

During this time, God worked miracles through Paul, causing many to magnify Christ.[14]

> God was performing extraordinary miracles by the hands of Paul...This became known to all, both Jews and Greeks, who lived in Ephesus; and fear fell upon them all and the name of the Lord Jesus was being magnified.[15]

God used Paul mightily to persuade many to turn to the Lord from idols.[16]

> You see and hear that not only in Ephesus, but in almost all of Asia, this Paul has persuaded and turned away a considerable number of people, saying that gods made with hands are no gods *at all*.[17]

This large-scale conversion caused a significant disturbance there. Ephesus, a key port city in Asia Minor, was noted for its commerce related to the worship of Artemis (or Diana in Latin), the premiere

---

[13] Acts 19:9-10.
[14] Acts 19:11,17.
[15] Ibid.
[16] Acts 19:26.
[17] Ibid.

goddess in Ephesian culture.[18] Paul's ministry created economic turmoil but resulted in a powerful advance of the gospel.[19]

So the word of the Lord was growing mightily and prevailing.[20]

Writing to the Corinthians from Ephesus, he observes that he had many battles at Ephesus, but at that present time the climate was ripe for the gospel – a wide door had opened for service there, still there were many adversaries.

If from human motives I fought with wild beasts at Ephesus, what does it profit me...But I will remain in Ephesus until Pentecost; for a wide door for effective *service* has opened to me, and there are many adversaries.[21]

Later, Paul sailed past Ephesus on his way to Jerusalem.

For Paul had decided to sail past Ephesus so that he would not have to spend time in Asia; for he was hurrying to be in Jerusalem, if possible, on the day of Pentecost.[22]

He called the elders of the church at Ephesus, and offered them a farewell of sorts, charging them with these words:

[18] Acts 19:18-20:1.
[19] Acts 19:20.
[20] Ibid.
[21] 1 Corinthians 15:32, 16:8-9.
[22] Acts 20:16.

> Be on guard for yourselves and for all the flock, among which the Holy Spirit has made you overseers, to shepherd the church of God which He purchased with His own blood.[23]

This exhortation was very similar to his later warning to Timothy while Timothy was ministering in Ephesus at Paul's direction:[24]

> As I urged you upon my departure for Macedonia, remain on at Ephesus so that you may instruct certain men not to teach strange doctrines...Pay close attention to yourself and to your teaching. Persevere in these things...[25]

Timothy was to fulfill a key leadership role in Ephesus, but his first responsibility was to guard himself. Later, Paul sent Tychicus to Ephesus,[26] perhaps as a follow-up to an earlier visit in which he may have delivered Paul's letter to the Ephesians.[27] In that letter Paul wrote to the Ephesian church, addressing specifically the faithful in Christ Jesus.[28] The letter gives indication that conditions in the church were encouraging, as Paul offered no correction, only encouragement, teaching, and exhortation.

The final direct Biblical references to Ephesus arrive roughly less than thirty years later, as John is told to write the book of Revelation and to send it to Ephesus and six other churches (Rev 1:11). That book contains a section specifically addressed to the church at Ephesus:

---

[23] Acts 20:28.
[24] 1 Timothy 1:3.
[25] 1 Timothy 1:3, 4:16.
[26] 2 Timothy 4:12.
[27] Ephesians 6:21.
[28] Ephesians 1:1.

To the angel of the church in Ephesus write: **T**he One who holds the seven stars in His right hand, the One who walks among the seven golden lampstands, says this: "I know your deeds and your toil and perseverance, and that you cannot tolerate evil men, and you put to the test those who call themselves apostles, and they are not, and you found them *to be* false; and you have perseverance and have endured for My name's sake, and have not grown weary. But I have *this* against you, that you have left your first love. Therefore remember from where you have fallen, and repent and do the deeds you did at first; or else I am coming to you and will remove your lampstand out of its place—unless you repent. Yet this you do have, that you hate the deeds of the Nicolaitans, which I also hate."[29]

The message includes a commendation for the church's deeds, toil, perseverance, discernment, and hatred of the same deeds that God hates. Sadly, they are indicted for a critical error: they had fallen from a lofty place, having left their first love. The Greek word translated *left* is *aphekes*, and is literally to *quit* or *give up*. The glorious Ephesian church closes out their Biblical history having abandoned their first love, and being given a stern mandate to repent – to change their minds, and remember from whence they had fallen. They started with a roar, and finished with a whimper.

It seems that the church at Ephesus had maintained a focus on doctrinal soundness, yet when we examine the *expected result* of doctrinal

---

[29] Revelation 2:1-6.

soundness, we might reconsider: "But the goal of our instruction is love from a pure heart and a good conscience and a sincere faith."[30]

*Love* is the predicate nominative, and the other three traits are describing the love: from a pure heart, from a good conscience, and from a sincere faith. The goal of sound instruction is, simply, love – the right kind of love. We understand that our order of priority in expressing love is for the Lord first, and then for each other. The result of sound teaching is love for Him and love for people.

> And He said to him, "YOU SHALL LOVE THE LORD YOUR GOD WITH ALL YOUR HEART, AND WITH ALL YOUR SOUL, AND WITH ALL YOUR MIND." This is the great and foremost commandment. The second is like it, "YOU SHALL LOVE YOUR NEIGHBOR AS YOURSELF." On these two commandments depend the whole Law and the Prophets.[31]

> Keep yourselves in the love of God, waiting anxiously for the mercy of our Lord Jesus Christ to eternal life.[32]

> Beloved, let us love one another, for love is from God; and everyone who loves is born of God and knows God…Beloved, if God so loved us, we also ought to love one another. No one has seen God at any time; if we love one another, God abides in us, and His love is perfected in us.[33]

---

[30] 1 Timothy 1:5.
[31] Matthew 22:37-40.
[32] Jude 21.
[33] 1 John 4:7, 11-12.

The threat we face, then, is not losing truth for truth's sake, but losing truth and in the process losing our love for Him. That is the very essence of idolatry. John warns believers of idolatry, saying, "Do not love the world or the things in the world. If anyone loves the world the love of the Father is not in him."[34]

His warning is clear, that believers can fall into the trap of loving the wrong things, and in so doing failing to love the Father. John is certainly not suggesting we should not love the people in the world, after all, he was present when Jesus exhorted His listeners to love their neighbor (in the story of the good Samaritan[35]). John also records that God loved the whole world,[36] and that Christ died for the whole world.[37] On the contrary, John is cautioning against the world system – the course of this world[38] and the things in that system that lead us astray – the lust of the flesh and the eyes and the boastful pride of life.[39]

If we are loving these things, then we are not actively loving the Father, and what a heartbreaking thing that is, for a child not to love their Father who loves them. Holding fast to the Biblical worldview is not about maintaining tradition nor even simply about upholding the institution's mission. The case study of the church at Ephesus underscores that the stakes are higher than all that.

---

[34] 1 John 2:15.
[35] Luke 10:29-37.
[36] John 3:16.
[37] Cf. 1 John 2:2, Romans 5:8.
[38] E.g., Ephesians 2:2.
[39] 1 John 2:16.

## PRINCIPLES FOR LONGEVITY
## FROM THE EPHESUS CASE STUDY

In considering some principles we can absorb from the failure at Ephesus, we realize that there is perhaps no church in the New Testament so advantaged as was the church at Ephesus. While we are not told specifically what factors led to their failure, we see clearly that within less than one generation they had walked away from what should have been their highest priority. The church at Ephesus offers a cautionary tale that all who would be involved in Christian leadership should carefully consider. In particular, there are seven key facts of the narrative that can help us assess how we can avoid the Ephesian error in our own institutions. First, the church at Ephesus was surrounded by and under constant threat of idolatry.[40] Second, leaders were warned of present dangers.[41] Third, the Ephesians had every advantage with excellent teaching and ministry, including by Paul, Timothy, and Tychicus.[42] Yet they were not too mature to fail. Fourth, leaders were given precise instructions for how to avoid the danger.[43] Fifth, leaders were warned to guard themselves *first*.[44] Sixth, leaders were warned to guard the flock.[45] Seventh, the Ephesians ultimately left their first love.[46] From these facts, we can ask some key questions facing leaders of Christian institutions. How we answer these questions tells us much about where we are on the continuum between faithfulness and failure.

---

[40] 1 Corinthians 16:8.
[41] Acts 20:28, 1 Corinthians 16:8, 1 Timothy 1:3.
[42] 2 Timothy 4:12.
[43] Acts 20:28, 1 Timothy 4:16.
[44] Ibid.
[45] Acts 20:28.
[46] Revelation 2:4.

First, what pressures and threats would cause us to quit our first love? If our institutions were to fail, what went wrong? If we can offer an objective post-mortem analysis before the failure takes place, then we have a much greater opportunity to avoid the tragic failure. This is one of the obvious advantages of a SWOT analysis.

Second, how are we warned of the present dangers? How does the Bible specifically warn us in light of the pressures and threats we face? Are there leaders or anyone in our institutions who are raising concerns? Are we listening?

Third, what advantages do our institutions have, and how have these advantages insulated the institutions from the looming specter of idolatry? Are these advantages making us complacent? If so, how?

Fourth, what specific instructions are we given for responding to the present dangers, and how can we apply those? For example, fiscal responsibility is a virtuous and necessary pursuit, but is there a danger of focusing too much on financial gain? If so, how does the warning of 1 Timothy 6:6-11 impact our fiscal policies – especially in light of the 1 Timothy 3:3 qualifications for leadership in the church?

Fifth, are we as leaders guarding ourselves first? Are we modeling what our institutions are trying to produce? Are we focusing on our own personal spiritual integrity and growth?

Sixth, are we as leaders guarding those we are leading? Are we protecting our constituency by making the right hires and retaining people who are committed to the same worldview core? Are we committed to academic models and student services that encourage quality spiritual life? Are we encouraging transformative growth at every level?

Finally, are we moving closer to or further from our first love? In short, we need to have the right priorities, and not focus solely on the mere survival of our institutions. These institutions exist for a reason, and not simply to continue to exist. Self-defense is not our highest calling.

The Ephesian failure invites us to consider ultimately whether or not we are willing to encounter failure in other areas (financial, popularity, respect in the academic community, etc.) in order to maintain faithfulness in what matters to God.[47] If we are unwilling to fail in unimportant ways, we *will* fail where it matters most. So, let's ask the seven questions we glean from the Ephesian failure, and honestly consider appropriate steps to guard ourselves and our institutions from leaving our first love.

---

[47] John 12:25.

# 14
# CONTINUOUS IMPROVEMENT
## KAIZEN AND THE BIBLICAL MODEL

Kaizen means *improvement*. Identified by author Masaaki Imai as "the key to Japanese competitive success,"[1] kaizen is the philosophy undergirding continuous improvement at every level of the organization, and involving all personnel. As a philosophy, kaizen is the post-World War II driving force behind the success of a host of Japanese companies, led most notably by Toyota.

Kaizen, as an organizational philosophy, was introduced to Japan through several American post-World War II initiatives designed to help war-torn Japan recover and flourish. W. Edwards Deming received an award from the Emperor of Japan for his involvement in developing and implementing kaizen. The W. Edwards Deming Institute remains a significant influence in continuous improvement, including in the promotion of the basic kaizen cycle (PDSA cycle) of plan, do, study, act:

> The cycle begins with the Plan step. This involves identifying a goal or purpose, formulating a theory, defining success metrics and putting a plan into action. These activities are followed by the Do step, in which the components of the plan are online

---

[1] Masaaki Imai, *Kaizen: The Key to Japan's Competitive Success* (New York: McGraw Hill, 1986), xxix.

slots implemented, such as making a product. Next comes the Study step, where outcomes are monitored to test the validity of the plan for signs of progress and success, or problems and areas for improvement. The Act step closes the cycle, integrating the learning generated by the entire process, which can be used to adjust the goal, change methods or even reformulate a theory altogether. These four steps are repeated over and over as part of a never-ending cycle of continual improvement.[2]

Especially creditable to Toyota's success, kaizen's popularity increased, and kaizen has since been implemented by noted companies like Ford, Great Western Bank, Lockheed Martin, along with an innumerable host of companies who have likewise benefited from the PDSA cycle.

Kaizen is clearly a positive change agent. But what is most interesting to this writer is how the philosophies of kaizen coincide markedly with quite a few Biblical principles. The similarities show that there is enough Biblical data to infer a Biblical model for continuous improvement (hereafter, BCI) – a model that can be very effective.

## PRINCIPLE #1: IMPROVEMENT REQUIRES HUMILITY, COLLABORATION AND ACCOUNTABILITY

Kaizen as a philosophy began with collaboration. General MacArthur invited some American quality control experts to help the Nippon Telegraph and Telephone Public Corporation resolve a

---

[2] The Deming Institute, "The Plan, Do, Study, Act (PDSA) Cycle," at https://www.deming.org/theman/theories/pdsacycle.

pervading wrong-number problem. "The American experts told NTT management that the only solution was to apply quality control…"[3] Hajime Karatsu (Technical Advisor to Matsushita Electric Industrial), aiding the NTT, recounts, "In our pride, we told them that we were applying quality control at NTT the Japanese way. But when they asked to see our control charts, we didn't even know what a control chart was."[4] What the NTT lacked was another set of eyes – an external accountability – to help them understand deficiencies and how to resolve them.

"A wise man will hear and increase in learning, and a man of understanding will acquire wise counsel."[5] "Where there is no guidance the people fall, but in abundance of counselors there is victory."[6] "Without consultation, plans are frustrated, but with many counselors they succeed."[7] "Listen to counsel and accept discipline, that you may be wise the rest of your days."[8] "For by wise guidance you will wage war, and in abundance of counselors there is victory.[9]" Solomon's words underscore the importance of humility, collaboration, and accountability if plans are to succeed.

Even within the church-age economy (recorded in the New Testament), success is never achieved individually, for "even as the body is one and yet has many members, and all the members of the body, though they are many, are one body, so also is Christ…For the body is not one member, but many… If the foot says, 'Because I am not a hand,

---

[3] Imai, 10.
[4] Ibid.
[5] Proverbs 1:5.
[6] Proverbs 11:14.
[7] Proverbs 15:22.
[8] Proverbs 19:20.
[9] Proverbs 24:6.

I am not a part of the body,' it is not for this reason any the less a part of the body. And if the ear says, 'Because I am not an eye, I am not a part of the body,' it is not for this reason any the less a part of the body. If the whole body were an eye, where would the hearing be? If the whole were hearing, where would the sense of smell be? But now God has placed the members, each one of them, in the body, just as He desired. If they were all one member, where would the body be? But now there are many members, but one body. And the eye cannot say to the hand, 'I have no need of you;' or again the head to the feet, 'I have no need of you.' On the contrary, it is much truer that the members of the body which seem to be weaker are necessary; and those members of the body which we deem less honorable, on these we bestow more abundant honor, and our less presentable members become much more presentable, whereas our more presentable members have no need of it. But God has so composed the body, giving more abundant honor to that member which lacked, so that there may be no division in the body, but that the members may have the same care for one another. And if one member suffers, all the members suffer with it; if one member is honored, all the members rejoice with it. Now you are Christ's body, and individually members of it."[10]

The author of Hebrews extols the necessity and advantage of collaboration: "and let us consider how to stimulate one another to love and good deeds, not forsaking our own assembling together, as is the habit of some, but encouraging one another; and all the more as you see the day drawing near."[11] In these words is embedded the BCI basis for collaboration and its advantage. *There is a day drawing near.* This

---

[10] 1 Corinthians 12:12, 14-27.
[11] Hebrews 10:24-25.

eschatological reference draws the reader's attention to a substantial distinction between kaizen and BCI; whereas kaizen is a vehicle designed for continually achieving right outcomes in diverse contexts, BCI *is* the outcome. Within a Biblical worldview, relationship-growth and maturing are not simply desired outcomes. Rather they are the stuff of everyday life, and everyday life should not be disjointed from the conclusion of it. The destination is the journey, as they say. In the words of one popular song,

> Just a closer walk with Thee
> Grant it Jesus, is my plea
> Daily walking close to Thee
> Let it be dear Lord, let it be.[12]

Improvement requires humility, collaboration, and accountability. Further, in BCI, improvement is more than becoming better at processes, it is *becoming better.*

PRINCIPLE #2:
OFTEN COMMON SENSE IS ALL THAT IS NEEDED.

While innovation usually requires highly sophisticated technology, kaizen often simply requires common sense.[13] Innovation is an event that brings steady deterioration as soon as it is installed, whereas improvement is a constant process. That is not to say that kaizen does not create innovation, rather innovation is not the primary

---

[12] "Just a Closer Walk with Thee," traditional gospel song, writer unknown.
[13] Imai, 25.

pursuit. Improvement is. Because of that emphasis, and the comprehensive involvement of all personnel, innovation can happen at any level. Imai's observation of Honda in the mid-eighties illustrates the point: "Technological breakthroughs in the West are generally thought to take a Ph.D. But there are only three Ph.D's on the engineering staff at one of Japan's most successfully innovative companies – Honda Motor. One is founder Soichiro Honda, whose Ph.D is an honorary degree, and the other two are no longer active within the company. At Honda technological improvement does not seem to require a Ph.D."[14] Kaizen companies dedicate resources to the people doing the actual work, so that innovation can happen at any point in the chain where it can contribute to improvement.

BCI is likewise rooted in right understanding. There is a Biblical common sense that is grounded in the right understanding of God. Rather than an independent rationalism, BCI relies on divine wisdom that is accessible by all, not just the elite. "Trust in the Lord with all your heart and do not lean on your own understanding. In all your ways acknowledge Him, and He will make your paths straight.[15]" The Proverbist adds, "The fear of the Lord is the beginning of knowledge,"[16] "The fear of the Lord is the beginning of wisdom, and the knowledge of the Holy One is understanding,"[17] and "the Lord gives wisdom; from His mouth come knowledge and understanding."[18] In this latter of these statements the root of right understanding is exposed: God's word is the source of knowledge, wisdom, and understanding, and the content

---

[14] Imai, 34.
[15] Proverbs 3:5-6.
[16] Proverbs 1:7.
[17] Proverbs 9:10.
[18] Proverbs 2:6.

of it is the fear of the Lord (or put another way, the proper evaluation of the Lord).

In the church-age economy this right understanding is not available only to the elite but is accessible to all who are in Christ: "Now there are varieties of gifts, but the same Spirit, and there are varieties of ministries, and the same Lord. There are varieties of effects, but the same God who works all things in all persons. But to each one is given the manifestation of the Spirit for the common good."[19] This passage describes how the Holy Spirit works in the body of Christ to enable each person to fulfill their tasks, and ultimately this is for the good of the entire body. Once again, no one is to function independently of the rest of the body, nor is success (faithfulness) an individual sport.

The common sense that drives BCI is not simply the elementary facts and figures of reality and human experience, it is rather the grounding of those facts and figures – the *undergirding* of what is known in human experience: "For by Him all things were created, both in the heavens and on earth, visible and invisible, whether thrones or dominions or rulers or authorities – all things have been created through Him and for Him. He is before all things, and in Him all things hold together."[20]

---

[19] 1 Corinthians 12:4-7.
[20] Colossians 1:16-17.

# 15
# PERSONALIZING THE GEMBA WALK

From the Japanese term deriving from *gembatsu*, and referring to "the real place," Gemba (or Genba) is a concept applied in several improvement and efficiency models *to understand through observation what is really taking place in the place where the work is actually being done*, and to collaborate with the people actually doing the work in order to help improve processes and results. Jim Womack describes the Gemba Walk as

> A horizontal journey along a value stream (a value creating process) across departments, functions, and organizations to facilitate: A transformational leap in performance…Sustainable improvement…Coaching the next generation…"[1]

Developed under the leadership of Talichi Ohno of Toyota, the Gemba Walk is a fundamental component in lean manufacturing, serving as a catalyst for improving processes and minimizing inefficiency. Gemba involves physically walking the space where the work is done and where the value is created, rather than simply analyzing data from a centralized location (conference room or the like).

---

[1] Jim Womack, "Gemba Walks" at Industry Week Best Plants Conference, Atlanta, Georgia, April 5, 2011.

The value of the Gemba Walk is evident in several ways. Firsthand knowledge is the best kind of knowledge – while Ohno valued data, he also recognized that data did not always tell the story. (1) Firsthand knowledge fills in important blanks. (2) People are more important than processes. Each person involved offers unique perspective on the processes, and it is important to remember that the processes are in place to help people fulfill their roles and not the other way around. (3) Perspective matters. Just as one cannot understand what a house is by simply looking at a materials list, it is difficult to really understand how the value is created simply from the data.

"Go see, ask why, show respect" – these famous words of Toyota Chairman Fujio Cho sum up the Gemba Walk process. "Go see" involves (1) viewing the Gemba in order to assess the alignment of the Gemba's purpose with that of the organization, (2) observing processes to understand whether or not they are designed to support the purpose, and (3) to engage the people to gain their perspectives on whether or not the processes are designed to help them fulfill their roles in achieving the purpose.

"Ask why" can be done from four perspectives, the solution view (which looks for opportunities to employ solutions), the waste view (which tries to identify areas of waste or inefficiency), the problem view (which starts with objectives, confirms design, and asks why the objectives can't be met), and the Kaizen view (which seeks to examine for improvement at a system level).[2] Each are valid and important in context (though this writer prefers the Kaizen perspective for its broad and systemic impact).

---

[2] John Shook, "How to Go to the Gemba: Go See, Ask Why, Show Respect," 6/21/2011, https://www.lean.org/shook/displayobject.cfm?o=1843.

"Show respect" is perhaps the most valuable piece, as people are the goal, not simply the means to an end. Womack suggests that the Gemba Walk is "to grasp the situation by involving everyone touching the process to understand purpose, process, and people."[3] Objectives are accomplished by people, not processes. Processes ought to be designed to support people in their accomplishment of objectives. Ultimately this means developing people to be who they can be. One tremendous side effect of that development is greatly increased capability in fulfilling their roles, which leads to greater efficiency in accomplishing objectives. The Gemba Walk is a visible way for leadership to invest in people *as people* and not merely as resources to be harnessed for organizational gain.

The Gemba Walk is intended to provide accurate self-assessment and organizational assessment through the lens of peers and organizational members; it relies on foundational truths and objectives to provide the basis for objective assessment; and it expects to facilitate transformational growth. In these three areas, the Gemba Walk bears remarkable similarity to the Biblical process of personal and organizational growth.

The Bible describes the importance of accurate self-assessment, both for the individual and for the group. The Apostle Paul recognizes that self-examination is limited in its effectiveness, and that accountability is needed in order to arrive at an accurate self-assessment:

But to me it is a very small thing that I might be examined by you, or by any human court; in fact I do not examine myself.

---

[3] Womack, "Gemba Walks."

For I am conscious of nothing against myself, yet I am not by this acquitted; but the one who examines me is the Lord.[4]

Paul understands that there is benefit in the perspectives of others, but ultimately he relies on the one perspective he knows to be fully trustworthy – the Lord's. Even though Paul may not find deficiency in himself, he recognizes that God's perspective is more accurate. The lesson here is the same that is put into practice in the Gemba Walk – accurate self-assessment requires objective accountability and candor from observers. Incidentally, this principle has great value in our personal lives. If Paul is correct, and God is the accurate Observer, then what God has to say about us should carry the greatest weight, and we should look to Him for our definitions.

When He describes the foundational truths that we are lost and lifeless without Him,[5] that He has provided for us to be remade with new life and purpose,[6] and that He has provided the empowerment and objectives for our transformational growth,[7] we ought to recognize that in the Gemba Walk of life, we cannot ignore the truth that is right in front of us.

With respect to the organizational aspects of accurate self-assessment, foundational truths and objectives, and transformational growth described in the Bible we need look no further than God's plan and purpose for the collective group of believers in Christ, often referred to as the church. In God's loving leadership of this group, we see the time-tested and divinely derived principles which the Gemba

---

[4] 1 Corinthians 4:3-4.
[5] Romans 3:23, 6:23.
[6] 1 Corinthians 15:2-3, Ephesians 2:8-10.
[7] Romans 12:1-2, John 17:3.

Walk more recently illustrates. First, all members of the group are placed in the group deliberately for an ultimate purpose and design.[8] They are given foundational truths and principles to guide them as they grow and function together.[9] They are empowered to achieve a grand purpose and to serve one another in the utilization of those empowerments.[10] Each member of the group is promised transformational growth if they engage faithfully in the process,[11] and are cautioned that if they ignore the process, that growth can be hindered,[12] even if their position as part of the group is secure.[13] In this journey, each member of the group is to "show respect" for one another.[14] Each member is to "ask why," holding each other accountable.[15] Each member is to "go see," engaging each other for accurate assessment and for seeking one another's highest good.[16]

The Gemba Walk is an enlightening tool for organizational leadership, and because it was crafted from timeless and divinely derived principles it provides more than an organizational tool. Develop a Gemba Walk habit in your own personal life, and discover what God thinks about you, about your objectives, about your processes, and about how you are interacting with Him and others. I think you will want to be part of His organization – the collective group of those who have believed in Jesus Christ. And if you already are part of that group, then allow that group to do the Gemba Walks with you, and be willing

---

[8] Ephesians 2:8-10, 4:11-12.
[9] 2 Timothy 3:16-17.
[10] 1 Corinthians 12:7, 1 Peter 4:10-11.
[11] Romans 8:28-30, 1 Corinthians 3:7-9, Ephesians 4:15.
[12] 1 Corinthians 3:1-3, Galatians 5:16-25.
[13] John 6:47, Romans 8:1,38-39, 1 Peter 1:3-5.
[14] Philippians 2:1-11, Ephesians 5:21.
[15] Colossians 3:12-17, 1 Corinthians 5:12-6:7.
[16] Hebrews 10:24-25, Philippians 2:3-5.

to do it with them. God provides the objectives, the processes, and the people. "Go see. Ask why. Show respect."

# 16
# LEADING IN CRISIS
## ADAPTIVE LEADERSHIP AND DURABLE AGILITY

COVID-19 has proven to be a catalyst for global change. The timeless principles of what is important doesn't change. But the method, the format, the pedagogy, the medium, the context, the technology – these things endure the constant of change, and in times of crisis, the pace of change can accelerate exponentially. COVID-19 has been an accelerant unlike anything we have seen since the arrival of the smart phone and since the tragedies of 9/11. We now live in a *post-pandemic world*, anticipating the next episode.

With Covid-19, this world has encountered the millennium's first swift and truly global health threat, and much has changed nearly overnight. Especially for organizations historically resistant to change (like higher education institutions, for example) this means painful but necessary and rapid reinvention in nearly every area of strategy and tactics. It still remains to be seen what changes might be temporary and what will be durable, and how organizations and their leaders must adapt in response to those changes. COVID-19 has changed the landscape, reminding us of foundational principles. Things will never be the same after this pandemic, and the emerging *new normal* demands we consider at least seven concepts for organizational effectiveness as our paradigms are encountering seismic change.

## 1. THE EVER-PRESENT THREAT OF MISSION DRIFT

While many things must change, *the main thing must still be the main thing*. Crisis management can sometimes cause us to take our eyes off of our mission. Mission drift can go undetected in times of crisis, when attention is shifted from institutional purpose and value to institutional survival. For any worthwhile organization, **the mission is priority one and then sustainability is priority two**. When mission and sustainability are conflated, the organization begins to lose its worth and failure is usually not far behind. Of course, many organizations faithful to their mission fail anyway due to unsustainability, but at least those organizations were worthwhile and served something greater than their own existence. Failure happens, and no organization is immune. But those organizations that are best equipped to thrive even in times of crisis are those that have a clear mission and value proposition, and that have teams engaging with those critical principles through transformational rather than transactional leadership.[1] *Crisis does not change the values to which our missions are tethered. Crisis simply tests the strength of the tether.*

---

[1] E.g., "in a crisis situation, transformational leadership behaviors are associated with higher levels of positive affect and lower levels of negative affect among team members, which in turn relate to higher resilience. These results are consistent with the argument that transformational leaders influence team members' feelings by envisioning a positive picture of the future, expressing confidence in team members' abilities to meet high expectations, and conveying shared values." S. Amy Sommer, Jane M. Howell, Constance Noonan Hadley, "Keeping Positive and Building Strength: The Role of Affect and Team Leadership in Developing Resilience During an Organizational Crisis" *Group and Organization Management*, 41 (2), April 2016, https://journals.sagepub.com/doi/full/10.1177/1059601115578027.

## 2. MOVIMIENTO ES VIDA[2]

While we may prefer a return to the old normal, after a crisis, things almost never return to their previous state. As one philosopher said, we cannot step twice into the same river. If we underestimate the durability of chaos that this pandemic and other change-catalysts like it represent,[3] then it is more likely that we will prepare poorly or fail to be proactive altogether. Organizational (and individual, for that matter) desire for normalcy can be a disability in the face of a durable chaos. A much more viable approach is to develop resiliency and agility for dealing not only with times of crisis but also for peacetime. Making the most of opportunities and good stewardship are best engaged with a culture of agility, and that culture is no longer optional.

While it is very difficult to be poised to respond to the kind of extreme market conditions that would necessitate 6.6 million jobless claims in one week alone,[4] agility or death is the new organizational reality, and it is not entirely new, for that matter. If its necessity wasn't obvious before, it most certainly is now. When COVID-19 limitations meant that Costco had to stop serving samples to customers, rather than see the employees of Club Demonstration Services lose their jobs, Costco re-tasked many of them to help with various responsibilities including in-store sanitation. While that wasn't sustainable long term, for roughly a month, Costco's agility helped many workers to continue

---

[2] A survival reference from World War Z, Directed by Marc Forster, Paramount Studios, 2013.

[3] See Scott Atran, "ISIS: The Durability of Chaos" in NYR Daily, July 16, 2016, https://www.nybooks.com/daily/2016/07/16/nice-attack-isis-durability-of-chaos/.

[4] As occurred the week ending March 28, 2020, per Department of Labor figures, https://www.dol.gov/ui/data.pdf.

to work much longer than they otherwise would have.[5] Organizations like this that exercised continuous agility and were able to anticipate and be proactive in implementing needed change – both offensive and defensive – were the most effective.[6] Managing *change management* is as important as change itself.

— Built-in agility for rapid change in expense cost models will be needed in anticipation of future disruptions. Budgeting for any possibility can include modular scaling of expenses in increments or blocks that allow for increases and decreases to be made quickly and with predictable levels of organizational disruption. Early estimates indicate a 40-50% reduction in consumer spending at this stage, and that will surely impact every budget.[7]

— Better preparedness for resiliency in the face of disruption and decline means better readiness for seizing opportunity. Creating and maintaining durable margin for growth and

[5] Brianna Sacks and Ryan Mac, "The Company That Handles Free Samples at Costco is Shutting Down Because of the Coronavirus," Buzzfeed News, April 2, 2020, https://www.buzzfeednews.com/article/briannasacks/costco-contractor-cds-free-samples.

[6] Andre de Waal and Esther Mollema, "Six courses of action to survive and thrive in a crisis," *Business Strategy Series*, 11(5), September, 2010: 333-339, https://www.researchgate.net/publication/254191864_Six_courses_of_action_to_survive_and_thrive_in_a_crisis.

[7] Sven Smit, Martin Hirt, Kevin Buehler, Susan Lund, Ezra Greenburg, and Arvind Govindarajan, "Safeguarding our Lives and our Livelihoods: The Imperative of our Time," McKinsey and Company, March 2020, https://www.mckinsey.com/business-functions/strategy-and-corporate-finance/our-insights/safeguarding-our-lives-and-our-livelihoods-the-imperative-of-our-time.

expansion means that organizations can take a posture of seeking out ways to enhance market positioning even in market decline.

## 3. COMMUNITY HAS FLIPPED

Until the social media boom, community was necessarily perceived as including a physically in-person element. The pandemic has especially altered that, necessitating social distancing and forcing new standards for what is acceptable community interaction. Technology is no longer nuisance nor mere add-on, as conferencing and interaction tools continue to be utilized to an unprecedented extent. While the pandemic has passed, attitudes regarding the importance of social distancing and guarding personal health will likely change social posture from seeking out in-person interaction to a more practical and perhaps safer approach using technology since even those who avoided social technology in the past have gotten a crash course and are now becoming comfortable. Perceptions of social responsibility have changed, and the current peer pressure to respond accordingly will have lasting effect (just look at how many people still wear masks long after mandates have subsided). Current criticism of those who aren't properly social distancing adds impetus for our understanding of the idea of "social" to be permanently changed.[8] It has been suggested that "Instead of asking,

---

[8] See for example, Todd Brock, "Florio: Dez-Dak workouts violate NFL stay at home orders, NFL should 'do something,'" CowboysWire, April 8, 2020, https://cowboyswire.usatoday.com/2020/04/08/dez-bryant-dak-prescott-workouts-violate-coronavirus-orders-league-should-do-something/.

'Is there a reason to do this online?' we'll be asking, 'is there any good reason to do this in person?' "[9]

— For higher education, for example, online synchronous *and* asynchronous pedagogy and delivery is no longer optional. Providing flexibility for the end user to receive instruction and guidance in the mode of their preference will be necessary for staying power.

— Working from home is nothing new, but thousands have now proved it can be effectively done in industries that previously shied away from the work at home paradigm. In many more cases than before, "being in the office" no longer necessarily includes the trappings of geography. Organizations will need to assess carefully when and what roles require physical presence and what can be accomplished online.

— Online resources for customer service will need to be comprehensive, as in some cases people still expect even their fast-food restaurant experience to be completely online. Because the market has proven that it *can* operate that way, consumers will expect that their service providers *must* operate that way.

---

[9] Deborah Tannen, "The personal becomes dangerous," *Politico*, "Coronavirus Will Change the World Permanently. Here's How" March 19, 2020, https://www.politico.com/news/magazine/2020/03/19/coronavirus-effect-economy-life-society-analysis-covid-135579.

— Traditional obstacles for online delivery of products (such as regulation of online education, medical services, and perhaps even voting) are quickly being removed by necessity, creating opportunity for those who can engage the technology well. Vendors are recognizing the gravitational pull of the market, and opportunistically ensuring that the tools are accessible.[10] The genie will not go back in the bottle, and organizations must function well *online* first.

## 4. EXPERTISE STILL MATTERS

In an age of fake news and misinformation, credible information is more difficult to recognize. With the democratization of information through technology, everyone can have a voice. The anti-intellectualism stemming from the democratization of information is countered in crisis – especially in times of pandemic, when people come to realize that novices can mislead and do great harm. Accurate information is vital, and expertise still matters, but this also means that the "authorities" will be afforded *more* authority.

— General education will still have value, of course, but the sciences and health industries continue to move to the forefront as market needs in those areas were particularly exposed during the pandemic. The publicly acknowledged

---

[10] Steven Blackburn, "55 free higher ed resources during coronavirus pandemic" University Business, April 7, 2020, https://universitybusiness.com/free-college-management-software-faculty-resources-coronavirus-covid-19?oly_enc_id=5912E4542589D3Z.

heroes of the day were those laboring in health service industries, especially. Organizations will need to recognize that the images of heroism are changing, and be able to reach their constituencies in these contexts, with powerful value statements, by meeting some needs related to these areas, or by at least employing the imagery in communications.

— While in some areas, regulation will decrease, freeing up enterprise to deliver online, in at least one other key area, regulation will greatly increase. Just as after 9/11, the Patriot Act and TSA regulations limited personal freedoms without overwhelming public outcry. Governmental enactment of authorities not seen in decades (e.g., shelter in place orders) were employed with little public concern for personal liberties. This underscores a society that has been well trained from the aftermath of 9/11 to prefer safety over liberty. Organizations must anticipate the areas in which regulatory reach and overreach might impact their functions and be prepared.

## 5. RESEARCH AND ASSESSMENT CYCLES ARE SHORTENED

The traditional *annual cycles* of data assessment are inadequate to meet the present informational need in a rapidly changing environment. Consumers are changing perspectives based on rapidly emerging information, and the faster the flow of information, the faster the changes. For example, eleven percent of high school seniors who were already planning to attend a traditional college or university in the Fall of 2020 changed their mind due to COVID-19, while twenty-five percent of those who planned to attend said that COVID-19 influenced their choice of which college to attend.[11] Further, forty-four percent said that it was highly likely their choice of college might change based on COVID-19.[12] Current college students are also changing their opinions based on issues related to COVID-19. Simpson Scarborough reports that forty-four percent of current college students have a lower opinion of their school than before the crisis.[13] These numbers underscore how fluid opinion forming and decision making is in this present era of disruption. Organizations which are able to acquire, contextualize, and apply information quickly are better able to understand the perceived needs of their constituencies and to respond accordingly.

—    With updates happening in real time and coming through many media (especially social media), consumer expectations of information flow have changed. It is no longer acceptable, for example, for organizational websites to operate as historical archives or as marketing vehicles, rather they must provide up to the minute content and contextualization of events for the benefit of the constituency in real time.

—    A remarkable sixty-four percent of high school seniors prefer to observe an online class and take a virtual campus

[11] Simpson Scarborough, Higher Ed and COVID-19 National Student Survey, April, 11, 2020, https://cdn2.hubspot.net/hubfs/4254080/SimpsonScarborough%20National%20Student%20Survey%20.pdf.

[12] Ibid., 14.

[13] Ibid., 20.

tour rather than visit in person. Organizations that have not retrofitted to offer their products and services in formats preferred by their constituency will simply lose market share. Understanding constituency habits, needs, desires, etc. must happen quicker than ever before.

— The manner of response to the data is equally as important as the data processing itself. Accepted modes of official organizational communication include social networks. Incorporating social media into web presence is important, with 3.8 billion social media users in 2020.[14] Finding ways to directly interact with constituencies in real time is critical. Social media is currently the most utilized vehicle, but the demand for live *interactive* video is rapidly changing how we utilize social media.

## 6. DEMOCRATIZATION OF ASSEMBLY IS HERE TO STAY

In recent decades we have seen the democratization of the arts and of information. Technology has enabled production and distribution tools to be more readily available. Anyone can put together a movie or record a multi-track song using the most basic of tools. In the same way, COVID-19 has forced alternative methods for assembling. Video conferencing is nothing new, but trying to connect hundreds and thousands or more in real time in *interactive* ways has presented new challenges and parented new tools.

---

[14] J. Clement, "Number of social network users worldwide from 2010 to 2023," Statista, April 1, 2020, https://www.statista.com/statistics/278414/number-of-worldwide-social-network-users/.

In the past, organizations whose product is heavily dependent on assembly have focused on in-person community, and whichever ones have been best equipped to attract the most people to their location have been able to grow the organizations as they grow their assemblies and thus their consumer base. Responding to market share decline since 2015,[15] the NFL has sought to expand its base from its core of 50–59 year-old males to especially target 20–29 year-old males and women of all ages. Networks have incorporated new technologies to engage audiences with additional features. At the core, the NFL is still a spectator sport, and COVID-19 has threatened the most core element of the sport. The NFL, for example, canceled a major draft event originally planned for Las Vegas and opted for an online alternative. How leagues like the NFL handle the new and necessary extreme of online community will help shape how smaller groups respond to similar challenges.

Churches have been particularly resourceful during the pandemic, as even those churches that had resisted broadcasting or livestreaming now have sufficient motivation to engage their constituency with technology. The implementation of technology that has taken many churches a generation to implement has been accelerated at an unprecedented pace. Just as it has been proven that people can be productive working from home, it has now been demonstrated that assembly can be accomplished in an online setting. Many churches have not seen their in-person attendance return to pre-pandemic levels, while overall, online interaction has increased.

---

[15] Jim Johnson, "A Look Inside the Modern Sports Fan: NFL vs. NCAA vs. MLB vs. MLB," *Huffpost*, December 20, 2017, https://www.huffpost.com/entry/a-look-inside-the-modern-sports-fan-nfl-vs-ncaa-vs_b_5a3a9ed9e4b0df0de8b061a3.

The tools that are now being implemented to convene assemblies online have enabled access to assemblies that were previously geographically inaccessible for most. Now a person can "attend" their favorite church service regardless of its location. Again, the technology is not new, but the current volume of participating churches is. The standard for assembly has changed, as has the perception of what community actually is. During the height of isolation, one person lamented to me "I miss humans." This sentiment and the isolation that gave rise to it offered a window of opportunity for those organizations of assembly to have incredible outreach possibilities, with an eye focused on engaging rather than simply communicating to constituencies.

—   Leaders of those organizations need to recognize that just as the democratization of the arts and information have dramatically changed how we interact with people and with media, the democratization of assembly (through technology now readily accessible and easily implemented) will likewise change how we meet in community.

—   There is a continued trend toward interactivity and away from what Friere referred to as the "banking concept"[16] of depositing information in learners. Communicators and educators (and thus organizational leaders) need to engage their constituency rather than simply talking at them. This writer advocates that as a necessary component of

---

[16] Paulo Friere, *Pedagogy of the Oppressed*, 30th anniversary ed. (New York: Continuum, 2005), 72.

transformational learning,[17] and suggests that the current environment provides fertile soil for innovation in facilitating that kind of *transformative engagement*. Even this concept is nothing new, as the writer of the epistle to the Hebrews exhorts that readers "consider how to stimulate one another to love and good deeds, not forsaking the assembling together as is the habit of some, but encouraging one another…"[18] Encouraging and stimulating – these are terms of *engagement*, not simply one-way communication.

## 7. COLLABORATION IS KING

One of Waal's and Mollema's five factors of high-performance organizations (HPO's) is "the presence of an open and action-oriented organizational culture. An excellent organization "promotes interactive internal communications ("an open dialogue") between members of the organization to ensure that open and continual exchanges of information take place both vertically and horizontally throughout the organization."[19] Internal collaboration has always been vital, as have external partnerships and cooperation.[20] Crises and pandemics heighten the need and the value of cooperative efforts. In the wake of SARS,

---

[17] Christopher Cone, *Integrating Exegesis and Exposition: Biblical Communication for Transformative Learning* (Fort Worth, TX: Exegetica Publishing, 2015), 45, 302.
[18] Hebrews 10:23-25a.
[19] Andre de Waal and Esther Mollema, "Six courses of action to survive and thrive in a crisis" in *Business Strategy Series*, 11(5), September, 2010: 333-339.
[20] For examples of how partnerships are impacting sustainability of Christian higher education institutions, see Christopher Cone, "The Disappearing Middle Class in Christian Higher Education," March 3, 2013, http://www.drcone.com/2017/03/13/disappearing-middle-class-christian-higher-education/.

Jonathon Schwartz and Muh-Yong Yen considered the importance of collaboration across various components of society in order to meet future pandemic threats, discovering that some of the most effective policies were those that "rely heavily on public participation."[21] In the United States during this pandemic, federal and local guidance stopped short of martial law, but included shelter in place orders that were largely adhered to by much of the population. While there were outliers who refused to participate, slogans like #stayathome helped to provide a common purpose – and perhaps even more importantly – a common practice to mobilize the public to combat the unseen enemy together by...not mobilizing.

Mark Athitakis highlights some of the collaborations between public and private sectors that are helping to meet the crisis,[22] observing that "the partnership conversation may need to be [even] more broad and urgent, focused on the needs particular members have right now."[23] The WHO, UNICEF, and CEPI are working together, as Elizabeth Cousens, WHO president announced, "There has never been a more global need for global cooperation. The COVID-19 pandemic shows us that we can all do our part to stop the spread."[24] What we see in recent

---

[21] Jonathan Schwartz and Muh-Yong Yen, "Toward a collaborative model of pandemic preparedness and response: Taiwan's changing approach to pandemics" Journal of Microbiology, Immunology, and Infection, 50 (2), April 2017: 125-132.

[22] Mark Athitakis, "Leading During a Pandemic: A New Normal For Partnerships" April 5, 2020, https://associationsnow.com/2020/04/leading-during-a-pandemic-a-new-normal-for-partnerships/.

[23] Ibid.

[24] World Health Organization, "WHO and UNICEF to partner on pandemic response through COVID-19 Solidarity Response Fund," April 3, 2020, https://www.who.int/news-room/detail/03-04-2020-who-and-unicef-to-partner-on-pandemic-response-through-covid-19-solidarity-response-fund.

high-level collaborations are strategies to help constituencies recognize the need to unite in one transcendent purpose against a current common enemy (COVID-19).

— It has been said that deadlines make contracts, and the urgency created by pandemic implies all sorts of unknown deadlines that can foster collaborative effort readily beneficial for involved parties. One obstacle to collaboration between organizations is the lack of agility that can plague organizations in peacetime when the need for elasticity is not so apparent. Another potential obstacle is institutional fear of uncertainty, but when that uncertainty includes potential scenarios that extend beyond tolerable pain thresholds the fear of uncertainty can actually be a catalyst for collaboration. Obstacles will always remain, but healthy organizations are able to overcome obstacles and partner in ways that are needed and beneficial.

— What is next? Part of wise oversight is recognizing what threats might be possible and preparing to meet those challenges, even the unlikely ones. Identifying what are the "transcendent causes" that are motivating current action and considering what those causes might be in the future is at least a helpful exercise if not a necessary investment. Considering what potential threats may be ahead is helpful in identifying partnerships that are mutually beneficial so they can be engaged *before* they are absolutely necessary.

## CONCLUSION

The pandemic has passed, though another will surely come at some point in the future. While we have some good data from which to operate, leaders have to face uncertainties. We simply don't know what will come in the near future.[25] As Solomon reminds us, we have to run full steam ahead into the unknown using our best attempts at wisdom and the counsel of the wise to guide us.[26] It is in these times that we can be assured of the unchanging certainty that *change will happen*. For those who care to look, there is confidence to be found in the knowledge that there is One who is not taken off guard as these events unfold.[27]

To lead an organization well demands that we consider how change will affect those in our charge, and that we maintain a durable agility to meet those changes. But before we can lead others to true peace in times of tumult, we must look to the Source of knowledge, wisdom, understanding, and well-being for our own individual sustenance. With Him, we can endure any trial and run any race with endurance, no matter how threatening and no matter how frightening.[28]

---

[25] Ecclesiastes 8:7.
[26] Proverbs 15:22.
[27] Psalm 46:1-3.
[28] Isaiah 40:28-31, Hebrews 12:1-3.

# 17
# ESTABLISHING VALUES, MISSION, AND VISION

Healthy organizations are deliberate about what they do. They are focused on mission fulfillment and plan well in order to achieve that mission. Their efforts now and their plans for future activity are based on accurate assessment of data and are prioritized carefully to ensure that the symphony of efforts prescribed in the strategic plan will lead to excellence in pursuit of the mission. Assessment and strategic planning work in concert. Effective planning is data driven, and good assessment techniques make the data usable for deliberate and effective planning. The Cycle for Excellence is a roadmap for effectiveness in assessment, contextualization, planning, budgeting, and execution.

**PLAN**
7. Gap Analysis          8. Set Overall Course
6. Review Objectives      9. Develop Strategies
5. Review Mission         10. Develop Goals
**CONTEXTUALIZE**         11. Develop Objectives
4. Communicate Results    12. Develop Metrics
3. Diagnose               13. Develop Action Plan
                          14. Finalize Plan
2. Analyze and Evaluate   15. Executive Review and Approvals
1. Collect Data           16. Communicate Plan
**ASSESS**                **BUDGET**
22. Communicate Progress  17. Develop Budget
21. Track Status          18. Executive Review and Approvals
20. Take Action           19. Communicate Budget
**EXECUTE**

CONTEXTUALIZE · PLAN · ASSESS · EXECUTE · BUDGET

THE CYCLE FOR EXCELLENCE

Figure 4: The Cycle for Excellence

Think of this cycle as a highway with an onramp. Before the cycle can be engaged there is important prework needed to ensure the organization is getting on the right highway. The organization first needs to establish its values, vision, and mission based on the *who* - the highest priority.[1] Transcendent purpose is vital. It's important, but it's not the basis or the core of what we do. We have to understand who we are, and to understand who we are, we have to understand who were designed by and who that person is. In Proverbs 1:7 and 9:10, for example, the great leader Solomon explains that the fear of the Lord is the beginning of wisdom and knowledge and understanding. Solomon prescribes that we need the proper perspective for and response to the Creator in order to be on the right path to understand and have wisdom and to gain knowledge interpreted correctly and used wisely. Wise strategic planning begins with the recognition of the *who* as the absolute highest priority. We have got to know who this is all about. We have got to know who we are. If you're starting with *you*, unless *you* are the transcendent entity in the entire universe, your path is going to be insufficient. If your highest ideal is not high enough, then the house you are building will be built on sand. It is important that we work from the understanding of the One who created us, and then of who He has intended us to be – who He's designed us to be.

The *what* is a framework of values, vision, and mission. The values are non-negotiable and are the core from which you will be operating. The vision communicates the kind of future that you're imagining when the pursuit of these values is fulfilled. The mission is what you are committed to doing to ensuring that vision is realized.

---

[1] See Chapter 2, "Don't Start With *Why*, Start with *Who*."

We begin with establishing the **values**. Identify what those highest ideals are. Three to seven is manageable. Identify what those transcendent truths are – those non-negotiable ideals that you are willing to stake your organization's very existence on. Establish those values collaboratively with the team. Examine examples of other entities' values and assess and critique those. Appreciate this process of looking at the work of others and learning from their experiences. Look at value statements and assess them. Are these *good* values? Are these actually values? Critique the work of others not for sake of being judgmental but for the sake of being teachable and learning from their examples. Evaluate the prioritization matrices of others, in order to help you solidify your own. Codify what is important to you.

Next, look at the end of the road. One day the journey will end. We all have a shelf life on this earth, and so do our organizations. We only have so much time to invest in these endeavors. That time will go fast, and it will end quickly. Regardless of what stage you are in the organization's lifecycle (or your own), take the time to look to the end of the story and consider what is truly non-negotiable. What is the core that needs to be accomplished for me to say I fulfilled what I'm supposed to fulfill?

For me personally those values are derived from a Biblical perspective. I'm seeking to walk in a manner worthy of the calling with which I've been called as a believer in Christ, and I'm trying to encourage others to do the same. Those are two non-negotiable values for me. The Biblical writers constantly point us to the future so that we can peer into the future and understand that the moves we're making now need to be motivated by the end game. The **vision** is simply what things look like when your endeavor is complete. What is the condition that you would hope to have created? For some this may seem too philosophical or theological, and I understand that. You're just thinking, "I have a business. I want to manage a business. I want to have an excellent business, and then at some point I want to sell and make some money," or "I just want to provide for my family and do something I enjoy." Those are fine, but remember that death comes unexpectedly. Your story is going to end at some point. It doesn't end when you sell your business. It doesn't end when you shut down your business. It doesn't end when you retire. It ends when you're finished using the tools that you've been given. So, what are you doing with those tools? Vision is that future glimpse of the condition you'd like to see when you have finished implementing your values. Write out that vision. What does it look like? Think of *It's a Wonderful Life*.[2] George Bailey is given the gift of seeing what life would be like without him. He sees the *opposite* of the kind of vision we are talking about. Bailey sees the absence of the fulfillment in the implementation of his values. What is being shown in that story is that his current state, as miserable as it seemed and as failed as it might have appeared, was really magnificent. Yet he couldn't see it. He had to be shown what it would look like if he didn't exist. Once he understood, he rejoiced. He had a totally different perspective. The vision you are crafting will allow you to look into the future, a future that's created by the implementation of your values. This is what you are going to strive for.

You are now armed with your non-negotiable values and that glimpse into the future. Now you've got to get from here to there. The distance between those two (your values and vision) is really your **mission**. How are you going to implement those values in a specific expression in order to create the condition described in your vision?

---

[2] Frank Capra, *It's a Wonderful Life,* Liberty Films, 1946.

What are you going to do? What is your enterprise? What is your endeavor?

Before you think organizationally, it is wise to consider the individual implications of these three ideas (values, vision, mission). If you're starting with the right *Who* with a capital "W" in this Biblical framework there's this thing called eternal life, right? The moment a person believes in Jesus Christ, that person is a new creation and has an entirely new life and a new purpose, which means they have new **values**. The **vision** is given for them as an individual because in this Biblical system God allows us to see what's coming. He even provides for us the personal **mission**: *what we're supposed to do in order to implement these values and see that vision take place.*

Establishing value, vision, and mission for the organization comes much more easily once a person has recognized these in their own lives. Of course, Jesus did not die for organizations. He did not provide eternal life for organizations or institutions or businesses or enterprises. He died for individuals – and we are accountable for what we do with that. In the same way you are responsible for your personal values, vision, and mission, it is also your responsibility to provide directives and that structure for this organization. It's a big task, and not to be taken lightly. If you start with the wrong *who* or your values are too small or they're not really universal then your foundation is going to be flawed. It doesn't matter how good the cycle of excellence is. It doesn't matter how excellent your assessment is. It doesn't matter how solid your strategic planning is. You may still be going the wrong direction. Because of the foundational nature of values, vision, and mission, this prework before getting on the onramp is vital. It's worth spending a lot of time on.

If you don't have values clearly delineated you can't arrive at a vision, because you don't know what future you should envision. You also won't have a mission specific task in order to implement these values to create that vision scenario. If these things aren't based on the right *who*, then you're not ready to start. You're not ready to launch. Do the prework and don't shortcut that process.

. Having established values, vision, and mission, there is still some more pre-work to be done. You have your values established. you have your vision – the future that you'd like to see as you implement those values. You have the mission that helps you move from these non-negotiable values to the desired future in the vision. You have that mission. Now, what are the **objectives** that your mission requires you to have? In specific terminology, how do you navigate that path? What is that path? The **objectives are the path to mission fulfillment**. Objectives are the milestones and the checkpoints. **Goals** would be subsets of objectives. Goals are the **shorter-term things you're seeking to accomplish in order to hit the objectives to ensure mission fulfillment.**

Your values are the first priority. Your vision is the second priority. Your mission is the third priority followed by your objectives and then your goals. We need to be adaptive and recognize that unless the Lord builds the house the one who labors does so in vain.[3] We must be agile and be responsive to our *Who*. We can't control the future. He can. Yet, He has given us stewardships and tasks to fulfill, and we are accountable for those.[4] As leaders we must discern and navigate the best path and shine light on it for those we are leading.

---

[3] Psalm 127.
[4] E.g., Matthew 25.

Values, vision, and mission need to be assessed regularly. You may discover you have values that you didn't record. You may discover that your vision needs to change. You may discover that your mission is not sufficient, or scenarios have changed where the mission needs to change. From time to time you may need to pivot. Your objectives are very much related to the execution of those things, and they are the milestones that are ensuring that on the day-to-day operation of your entity you are fulfilling your mission. Objectives are not ethereal, philosophical, theoretical concepts. They are the nuts and bolts of the machine. Establishing measurable and attainable goals are key to achieving objectives. Well-designed objectives are critical for achieving the mission. A well-executed mission can facilitate the accomplishment of the vision. The vision reflects the values that are being expressed and promoted as ideal.

# 18
# STRATEGIC PLANNING

Once values, vision, and mission are established and codified, the organization can onramp to the cycle. The Cycle for Excellence is an ongoing and repeating sequence for continuous improvement and sustained focus. The cycle begins with assessment based on data, then contextualizes the data so that it can be understood and applied. A process of planning is engaged to respond to the data and the results of the analysis. Once the plan is established, a budget is formulated so that stakeholders can understand the financial needs, actions prescribed, and implications of the plan. Then the plan can be executed. Rinse and repeat. Assess, contextualize, plan, budget, execute.

**PLAN**
7. Gap Analysis
6. Review Objectives
5. Review Mission
**CONTEXTUALIZE**
4. Communicate Results
3. Diagnose
2. Analyze and Evaluate
1. Collect Data
**ASSESS**
22. Communicate Progress
21. Track Status
20. Take Action
**EXECUTE**

8. Set Overall Course
9. Develop Strategies
10. Develop Goals
11. Develop Objectives
12. Develop Metrics
13. Develop Action Plan
14. Finalize Plan
15. Executive Review and Approvals
16. Communicate Plan
**BUDGET**
17. Develop Budget
18. Executive Review and Approvals
19. Communicate Budget

THE CYCLE FOR EXCELLENCE

ASSESS

## 1. Collect Data

Collection of data is a constant. Even before one establishes their values, they are collecting data. Determining and evaluating values, vision, and mission requires data. The cycle requires initial data whether pertaining to the bases for deciding on values, vision, and mission or even to a simple inventory of progress. Because data collection is so critical, it is best if we pull from every available source and collate and store data in a way that can be easily accessed and utilized.

In order to avoid paralysis by inundation, prioritization of data is as important as data collection itself. For example, for those operating from a Biblical worldview, the Bible is the foremost source for decision-making rationale and prioritization matrices and undergirds the appropriating of acquired data. Utilizing the Scriptures to establish values, vision, and mission may seem obvious, but those same Scriptures provide light to our path as we work through the entire Cycle of Excellence and pursue mission fulfillment.

While our starting point in data collection may be well defined, we find less definition as we consider all other available sources. We must put in place tools for collecting internal data, whether from transactions, personal engagements, instances, or any reasonably measurable phenomena. We also ought to be outward looking as well, seeking external data that will help us pursue excellence. Seek counsel, continue education, look at financial data, look at demographic data, look at market data. Collect. Collect. Collect.

## 2. Analyze and Evaluate

One helpful way to utilize data is a **SWOT analysis**. SWOT is an acronym for **strengths, weaknesses, opportunities, and threats**. Strengths are internal positive qualities currently possessed. Weaknesses are internal negative qualities currently possessed. Opportunities are external advantages and positive possibilities. They're not strengths currently possessed. Rather they are strengths in the marketplace or strengths that we might be able to access. Threats are external disadvantages and negative possibilities. Threats can be negative market forces that threaten the organization's ability to fulfill its mission. While strengths and weaknesses are somewhat controllable by the organization (as they are internal), opportunities and threats are less controllable (being external), but must also be addressed and leveraged.

## 3. Diagnose

By diagnosing based on our analysis and evaluation of the data we have collected, we can begin to understand needed action points. We are identifying problems and beginning to uncover methods that can address and combat those problems. Based on collection, analysis, and diagnosis, we will establish hypothetical objectives and goals at first. Then we will test those as we continue through the cycle. The goals are established to achieve objectives. While there may be many ways to complete an objective, the process of data collection, analysis, and diagnosis help us to be most effective in goal creation. The idea is to be efficient in fulfilling objectives – to take the best path, if possible. Effective diagnoses help us arrive at good hypotheses, and good hypotheses make for good goals. We need to be able to counter those weaknesses that we have identified. We need to accurately diagnose what is needed, and then we need to identify an objective and then the goals to reach that objective. We are establishing goals based on analysis, based on data.

## 4. Communicate Results

All the data in the world is not going to help your team if they don't have access to it. You've heard the phrase "need to know basis." Burn that phrase. Write it in your notes and then burn your notes. Allow access to information so your team can see the broad context. Otherwise they don't have the big picture and can't contribute to the process beyond their own immediate context. Your organization needs your team to be informed, to be empowered, to have the information, to arrive at decisions. The less you inform your people, the less you communicate the results, the data, the analysis, the evaluation, the diagnosis – the less they're going to be able to help you. This is a challenge because the process of collecting data, analyzing, evaluating, and diagnosing is a lot of work. It takes a lot of time – a lot of bandwidth, and if everybody is doing that, less is getting done. However, if nobody's doing that except you, then little is getting done because your people don't have the data-based guidance they need. There are appropriate limits, of course, but always err on the side of informing and providing access. Develop a posture of communicating unless you have a specific reason not to, rather than not communicating, unless you have a specific reason to. Communicating results helps everybody to understand what the real information and the real evaluations are. Your team is then able to help with diagnoses and solutions. The team can better understand what drives goals and they can work to help you arrive at better goals.

## CONTEXTUALIZE

Once we have developed hypothetical goals, we need to develop metrics and measurements based on these goals and objectives. If we have a plan but we don't know how we're going to assess it and we don't build assessments into that process, then we're going to end up not being able to reshape our goals or objectives. We won't know whether we're being effective or not. So anytime we have an objective or goal we've got to have an associated metric. We need to measure whether we're hitting this goal or objective, and to do that we have to start with contextualizing. We need to understand the context that we're working in. We need to put the data into proper context so that we don't diagnose the wrong problem. We need to see the problem with the data in its context so that when we begin to take these next steps which will shape the organization, we do so based not only on data but *contextualized data.*

Here's an example I often use when teaching hermeneutics (or the interpretation of written communication). Psalm 14:1 says, "There is no God." If I don't recognize the surrounding context, I might conclude that the Bible teaches there is no God. It is a true statement that the Bible says there is no God. But I need understand the statement it in its proper setting. What immediately precedes those words is, "The fool says in his heart..." That makes the overall statement completely different. Context matters. In the same way, we are taking that data that we have collected; we're analyzing and evaluating it; we're diagnosing based on it; we're communicating the results. Now we need to…go back to the mission.

## 5. Review the Mission

The process of assessment enables us to evaluate the gap between our values and our vision. The means of getting from our values to their implementation in our vision is the mission. We may never actually change the mission, but every time we work through this cycle, if we are not reevaluating the mission then we are guaranteeing that at some point we will have an archaic organization. If our mission becomes antiquated or there are certain market conditions that change what the mission should be, and we are not looking at it constantly, then we have no hope of adjusting. Education provides a great case study for this. Twenty years ago, what we're doing right now was unheard of. This kind of distance learning and using technology in this way didn't exist. Some of the goals and the objectives might have included dealing with print manuscripts for notes or setting up classrooms for students to be engaging without the use of any technology. In time, a mission might need to change to accommodate new opportunities. For example, a school might need to include in their mission "using the most current technology." Perhaps innovation needs to be part of the mission. If we are not making use of the technology available, then we are not really making education accessible.

## 6. Review the Objectives

Reviewing the mission is important. More than likely you're not going to change your mission. But that mission will have pressure every four or five years because market conditions and other key factors do change. Review the mission and change it when it needs changing. Once the mission is (re)solidified, then move on to your objectives. Recall that in this system objectives precede goals. Objectives are the major milestones toward your mission. Your goals are the nuts and bolts – the shorter term, smaller step ways to achieve those objectives, and your objectives are ensuring mission fulfillment. So now you review your objectives. You're going back a step. If we change the mission then we certainly have to change the objectives. If we don't change the mission we still need to review and assess the objectives, as there might be better objectives we can develop to propel us toward mission fulfillment. Are the current objectives still in line with the mission? We are asking this question while looking at the context – the current status, the current data, the evaluations that we've done, and the diagnosis. We are involving others in those processes at least by communicating results. This expands our teamwork.

## 7. Gap Analysis

Next, we do a gap analysis. One element of gap analysis is to look at the gap between our values (non-negotiable universal principles upon which we're basing this organization's existence) and the vision. The gap between those two *ought* to be your mission. Your mission ought to bridge that gap. At this next stage we are looking at the **gap between our objectives and mission fulfillment**. Another way to say that is, we're looking at **the gap between what we say we do and what we actually do**. What we actually do is measured in whether or not we're meeting our objectives. What we say we do is the mission. What's the gap between the two? The entire process of strategic planning is designed to take that gap and reduce it, if not eliminate it altogether. That's what strategic planning is all about – identifying the gap between the mission and the actual engagement of the entity and eliminate the gap between the two so that you are actually fulfilling your mission. If we are doing that, then our strategic plan is being fulfilled and our mission is more within reach.

We've got our context. We've reviewed the mission. We are confident we've got the right mission. We've reviewed the objectives that we have, connected them again to the mission, and now we're taking all that data in the diagnosis and we're doing an analysis of the gap between what we're actually doing and what our mission is. The gap analysis tells us what our plan needs to be. Then we begin the planning stage, and that would be specifically steps eight through sixteen of the cycle.

PLAN

**8. Set the Overall Course**

First we need to set the overall course. From the results of our gap analysis, we identify what we saying we are doing but aren't actually doing. We itemize where we are missing the mark. We may discover we are not hitting our objectives, or our objectives don't align with our mission any longer because we changed our mission. Now we have to change our objectives, and our gap is even bigger. Or we may find that we adjust our mission and our objectives, and the gap is smaller. In this case, perhaps the problem is we've had the wrong mission all along for what we're really set up to do. Perhaps we've been aiming in the wrong direction. We're equipped to do something different so let's change our mission. We need to recalibrate our overall course. (Re)establish the mission, (re)evaluate the objectives, and put in place hypothetical goals. Now, it is time to develop strategies to meet the gap between our objectives and our mission fulfillment.

## 9. Develop Strategies

Now we begin to develop strategies and tactics to meet the gap, and we don't yet know whether those strategies and tactics are related to objectives or to goals. In this approach, strategic thinking pertains to the objective level, while tactics are more detailed and precise, targeting the goal level. At this point we will first deal with tactics and goals. Then we will return to broader strategies for our objectives.

In the contextualization stage we have already looked at mission, objectives, and goals in their proper sequence. Now we want to reverse engineer objectives and goals, and look at the fit to see where we need adjustment and perhaps compromise.

## 10. Develop Goals

We need achievable and measurable goals to achieve objectives. If the goals can't be met, the objectives won't either. We're trying to reverse engineer to kind of meet in the middle if needed. We have broad strategies which will end up being objectives or related to objectives. We develop goals based on those hypothetical strategies. These goals are the more detailed and smaller task segments, and we are hoping to develop a fit between our goals and objectives so that we can finalize our objectives (step eleven).

## 11. Develop Objectives

Once we have achievable and measurable goals, we can begin to solidify the objectives. How easy this step is can be an indicator of how well we have assessed our data. If we have assessed the data well, reviewed our objectives well, and done a quality gap analysis, then our big picture thinking and our detailed process align as an internal check and balance. Our hypotheses are being proven out (or disproven and reframed) in our process. At this point we move forward, or we go back and reassess depending on what our process reveals. If our goals and objectives fit with each other, then we are on the right track. If not, we have more assessment, contextualization, and gap analysis to do.

## 12. Develop Metrics

We need to develop the tools of measurement so that we can employ them when we collect and assess the data in the next cycle. We're going to put in place tools for assessment. By what metric would we measure that we are accomplishing the objective or the goals? As has been said, a goal without a metric is simply a dream. We have to be able to do the assessment so that we can turn the dream that we're pursuing into something that's actually attainable and achievable. Develop metrics. Quantitative tools are most helpful – statistics and surveys, especially. Determine what tools to use based on what is being measured.

## 13. Develop the Action Plan

Once we have our mission, our objectives, our goals, and our tools to measure success or failure we can develop the action plan, often referred to as the strategic plan. All the previous steps of assessment, contextualization, and planning are designed to help us develop a solid, data-based strategic plan. This plan should be governed and populated by the processes that preceded it. The strategic plan should state the objectives. It should highlight goals leading to those objectives, and it should demonstrate clear mission alignment throughout.

The strategic plan should include specifics regarding who is accountable and responsible for each goal and objective. A goal without an owner will never be met. The plan will (in its final iteration) also include budgetary impact. A sample strategic plan section might look like this:

| Department and Person Responsible: | Accounting / CFO | | |
|---|---|---|---|
| Pertinent Objective | Specific Goal | Targeted Date | Budgetary Impact |
| 1.1 Develop and implement audit protocols to ready the organization for initiation of annual financial audits | 1.1a  Select and implement an accounting software conducive to departmental needs and structure. | March 4 | $23,000 |
| | 1.1b Write an SOP for Accounting staff to use system and prepare for annual audits. | May 16 | $2,400 |
| | 1.1c Train Accounting staff in SOP and the new system. | October 2 | $1,600 |

## 14. Finalize Action Plan

As the action plan is developed there will likely be numerous revisions and adjustments. It is important to put in place a deadline to complete the plan. With such an important aspect of an organizational schema, it is easy to turn a short process into a long one. Developing a process for finalizing the plan – even if not ideal – is healthy and helpful. It is better to have an OK plan in place than to have an excellent plan that never sees the light of day. Beware of the temptation to make it perfect. There is no such thing. Finalize your plan and then move on.

## 15. Executive Review and Approvals

Depending on its structure, an organization will need to have a system for executive review and approvals. Especially in non-profits or organizations utilizing teams and high levels of delegation, the action plan won't necessarily be created at the executive level. Ideally, many are contributing to the plan. In those cases, collaboration and review is vital. In many settings, the strategic plan would be approved by a board of directors, advisors, or an executive or ownership team. The review and approve stage provides a great opportunity to strengthen consensus and unified thinking and activity.

## 16. Communicate the Plan

We can have the best plan in the world, but if our team doesn't know about it, then we won't be able to achieve the plan. By this time there should already be significant tools for communication in place, but we can't take communication for granted at this or any other stage. Simply put, if we don't communicate the plan well, then nobody knows what's going on. The team might be going in many different directions like scattershot. If we have effectively communicated the results of our assessment (as in step four), then we are in a good position for the team to receive communication at this point. They will have the context for the plan, and hopefully we have had them involved all along the way. Ultimately, the plan should really present no surprises to the team that is engaged. Once the plan has been developed and communicated, it is time to formalize the budgetary impact of the plan.

## BUDGET

### 17. Budget

While it may seem counterintuitive to build a budget *after* building the action plan, it is critical that the plan comes before the budget. The budget is based on the plan, and not the other way around. Planning based on a budget is a recipe for failing to achieve the mission. We build a plan and then budget for the plan. If we can't accomplish the goals in the plan for budgetary reasons, then use that data to go back and adjust the objectives and goals. If we start with a budget, then we have short circuited the entire planning process. Of course, limited revenue means limitations in many areas of conducting business, but we need to let the mission dictate the objectives and goals, and then budget based on those. Especially when working in that order, we will be able to see real organizational progress toward mission fulfillment. It is simply a matter of prioritization and not skipping steps that would otherwise make us better.

### 18. Executive Review and Approval of Budget

In the same way the plan was finalized, reviewed, and approved, the budget should be handled as well. Involving the same team members allows for closing the loop, showing the team that processes are begun and completed, and that the organization is ready for action. Organizational follow-through creates momentum and promotes unity.

At a more basic level, engaging the review process helps address important questions one more time in this cycle. Are your objectives too

172 LED BY A LION

great? Are your goals, your timelines too short? Then again executive review and approvals are working through that process to collaborate and ensure you have a budget that meets the needs and has the buy-in that the organization needs to have.

## 19. Communicate the Budget

Very few businesses and entities will share entire budgets with their teams outside of board and executive contexts. Sharing that level of information has its challenges to be sure. But as I have emphasized previously, I will emphasize again: err on the side of sharing information and empowering your entire team. If you choose not to share the entire budget, at least share enough that you are closing the loop with the entire team. You communicated the assessment results (step four). You communicated your action plan (step sixteen). Now communicate the budget – at least in summary. This allows your people to be involved in and aware of the entire process. You don't have to share some key specifics (individual wages and earnings, for example) But by communicating a budget, you're showing that leadership is accountable. You are telling your team what decisions have been made about what the organization plans to do and how the organization is spending money. If you have communicated well throughout the cycle, your team will recognize the consistent transparency and have a good feel for the organizational culture. Communication helps you get buy-in form the team. But even if you don't have buy-in necessarily, you have at least been transparent. That will help when you get back to assessment.

Are our people really on board with our mission? Our mission leads to our objectives and our objectives lead to goals. If our people aren't in on the goals, they're not in on the budget. They're not connecting somehow. Perhaps it is a training opportunity. Perhaps we need to do a better job in training and helping them understand our process and where we're going.

At this point, strategic planning – including budgetary impact – is complete for the cycle. It is ideal to communicate the plan and budget at an end (or beginning) of fiscal year meeting. Introducing the next year's plan before the next year actually begins is perhaps better; that way no time is wasted, and the team is ready for the next steps. You are preparing the team to get on the Autobahn and your communication is an onramp of sorts. Prepare them for the jarring acceleration they might experience. Moving toward the execution of a plan is a difficult process and you want people prepared to be on that fast track with you.

## EXECUTE

### 20. Take Action

We have a plan in place, and it has been well communicated. It is time for execution. People are fulfilling the processes (the tactics), to achieve the goals, in order to meet the strategies and achieve the objectives. The desired outcome is mission fulfillment.

### 21. Track Status

As we are executing the plan, we are appropriately applying the work we did in step twelve (Develop Metrics). Tracking the team's status applies the metrics and measures progress in an ongoing way. It can be as simple as providing and discussing a monthly profit and loss statement so that the team can look at a financial metric. Perhaps you provide more in-depth financial data if appropriate. Perhaps you are circulating web traffic or user stats. There are available metrics for most industries. It may be challenging to get some of the info you might need, but be persistent, because tracking status through the measures you put in place is critical for your organization's ongoing health, sustainability, and ultimately mission fulfillment. If I'm not tracking the status of my activities, I may as well be driving with no headlights at night. I may be going in the general direction of the plan and working towards the goals, but I can't see the road in front of me. I don't really know where we are. I am driving blind. On the other hand, if we understand where we are, what our status is, what our progress is, we can adjust as needed. The building blocks of our plan can be adjusted as we are going. But of course, that requires excellent communication.

## 22. Communicate Progress

Just as in previous steps of the cycle, communication is critical. The better we are at communicating the organization's progress (and lack thereof), the better our team will be at helping us adjust and adapt to the challenges we are encountering. A good plan has built in agility. But sometimes things change so quickly that the plan needs to change quickly too. Without good communication, there is no organizational agility. The team is working toward the same goal – mission fulfillment. When the goals and objectives need to change, people need to know and understand why. Often this allows them to participate in developing solutions. This is the kind of adaptive leadership and durable agility that leads to organizations effectively fulfilling their mission. This allows us to fulfill the cycle and start again with assessment as we seek for the well-being of our team and the healthy function of our organizations.

# 19
# ORGANIZATIONAL ASSESSMENT

In the previous chapter we walked through the Cycle for Excellence. One of the crucial components of that cycle is ongoing assessment. As the cycle ends with evaluation and communication of progress, it begins anew with continued assessment based on protocols and metrics installed throughout the cycle. There is quite a variety of excellent tools for organizational assessment, and it is recommended that the organizational leader be aware of and utilize those tools as they fit the organizational context and need.[1] In this particular space, I want to return to a very basic tool – the SWOT analysis. Earlier we discussed the SWOT analysis with relation to personal growth, now we want to consider this approach as a point of entry to the world of organizational assessment.

As we close the loop on our first periodic implementation of the Cycle for Excellence, we return to assessment. We go back to step one. We have to assess with the metrics that were developed within our

---

[1] Some resources for identifying assessment toolkits include: William and Flora Hewlett Foundation, Informing Change, "A Guide to Organizational Capacity Assessment Tools: Finding and Using the Right Tools for the Job," at https://hewlett.org/wp-content/uploads/2017/11/A-Guide-to-Using-OCA-Tools.pdf; National Council of Nonprofits, "Organizational Self Assessments" at https://www.councilofnonprofits.org/tools-resources/organizational-self-assessments; Fieldstone Alliance, *A Funder's Guide to Organizational Assessment: Tools, Processes, and Their Use in Building Capacity* (Fieldstone, 2005); Roger Kaufman and Ingrid Guerra-Lopez, *Needs Assessment for Organizational Success* (Association for Talent Development, 2013).

plan. If we haven't gotten metrics built into our plan we can't track our status, and we certainly can't collect data. Where are we going to get the data at this point? It may have been fairly easy to collect data the first time because we initially use external sources (demographics, segment statistics, etc.). We may have our values, our vision, and our mission in order, but once we've done business for a cycle (usually that would be a year) if we haven't developed a way to develop and measure our own data then we may as well be starting over. We must assess our organizational capacity using the metrics that we put in place with our strategic plan. While very basic, the SWOT analysis can help us contextualize and apply the data.

The SWOT analysis considers data to understand organizational strengths, weaknesses, opportunities, and threats. The strengths are internal advantages; weaknesses are internal disadvantages. The opportunities are external advantages, and the threats are external disadvantages. Here's a very practical way to approach a SWOT analysis. First, using the data available to you (surveys, statistics, etc.), you're going to identify three of each. You may find this step to be easy, as the data and their implications jump off the page. Internal data will provide you an excellent framework for arriving at a reliable list of strengths and weaknesses. Your organization is what it is, and the data will show that. On the other hand, when you begin to consider opportunities and threats you may find it much more difficult, because those will rely on external (and perhaps more subjective) market data. We need to be able to exegete the culture a bit here, or at least the marketplace.

Let's consider some examples. During the COVID-19 pandemic, many churches in America largely shut down. People weren't coming to the campuses and to the church buildings. That sure looked like a threat – an external disadvantage. This was not necessarily reflecting weakness in the organizations (though some might certainly debate that point). People were being restricted whether rightly or wrongly, and they weren't going to church in the traditional manner. COVID-19 and the accompanying regulations were threats. But COVID-19 would also be an opportunity. Many churches in America had only minimally utilized technology. But even some of the most old-school assemblies realized they couldn't connect with their people unless the churches used the technology that the people were using in their everyday lives. These churches were forced almost overnight to pivot into embracing technology. The pandemic and related conditions presented an opportunity for these entities to step into the next generation, and many were able to see increases in the number of people they were engaging. There are quite a few lessons to learn from this, but in this specific context, it is an example of the principle that every threat can potentially present an opportunity.

Whether looking at strengths, weaknesses, opportunities, or threats you want to again connect them to the values, vision, and mission. How close are you to achieving this vision? How does the strength, weakness, opportunity, or threat make things more or less achievable? Maybe you need to adjust your vision. Maybe you need to adjust your mission. So you apply each of these to the *how* which is driving your mission.

For example, consider a SWOT analysis of Amazon.[2] Their first observed **strength** is a strong brand. That would seem to go without saying, but Amazon has diligently developed that over the years. It wasn't always that way. Another strength is moderate and expanding

---

[2] From Business Strategy Hub, "Amazon SWOT 2022: SWOT Analysis of Amazon" March 27, 2022, viewed at https://bstrategyhub.com/swot-analysis-of-amazon-amazon-swot/.

business diversification. I would suggest that they might be a little bit further along than simply moderate and expanding. They are positioned to be in virtually any industry they choose, and are definitely diversifying and even monopolizing. They have a high capability for rapid technological innovation, especially in online services. Why? Because they value online services and have determined to be the industry leader. They're beginning to define with AWS how business is done. They've been very effective in that.

Amazon's **weaknesses** include an imitable business model. When an organization is first to market and is diverse in its developments, someone else may be able to focus more narrowly and move in on a concept you have already proved. You're demonstrating this can work. This can be accomplished. You've shown everyone the recipe, and someone else will try to go and do it. Anything you do that is excellent in your organization will draw attention and others will imitate it.

Another weakness identified is that Amazon has limited penetration in developing markets. Surprisingly, there are emerging markets that Amazon has not yet penetrated. There's opportunity there but it is identified as a weakness because Amazon hasn't yet developed that. Another of their weaknesses is a limited brick-and-mortar presence. So, what do they do? They acquire a grocery chain, and they launch distribution centers all over the country to shore that up.

Their **opportunities** include expansion in developing markets. You see that happening. Amazon has global markets and a global distribution model that seems very effective. There are further opportunities for expansion of brick-and-mortar business operations, and they seem to be actually developing those, especially with the rapidly advancing distribution center concept. They are developing new partnerships with other firms especially in developing markets recognizing they don't have to do this all themselves. They can work with other partners.

Yes, believe it or not, Amazon has to also deal with threats – external disadvantages – just like everyone else. This includes aggressive competition with online and non-online firms. Walmart has not given up on the consumer goods category, and there are many smaller competitors who own significant chunks of market share. So what does Amazon do? They open up their distribution model and tools to small businesses. Now many small businesses are running their transactions through Amazon's distribution. Amazon has had a brilliant response to market threats. They turned a severe threat into an opportunity for new partnerships with other firms, especially in developing markets.

Cybercrime is another threat Amazon faces. If a great deal of Amazon's business is online and they're shut down, how many millions of dollars per second of sales would they lose? Amazon has jumped into owning the online services space in part to ensure the security of its own endeavors and then to build a profit center serving those who want the same type of security for their own businesses. Amazon's SWOT provides a useful case study demonstrating that no organization is so big or powerful that it isn't subject to the same weaknesses and threats as everyone else. As the apostle Paul once said, "Let him who thinks he stands take heed, that he does not fall."[3]

As a helpful exercise in preparing for an organizational SWOT assessment, read Paul's letters to the Thessalonians and to the Corinthians. Think in terms of a SWOT analysis as if you are a consultant working for these two organizations/churches and you're

---

[3] 1 Corinthians 10:12.

trying to help them grow. What are the internal advantages – the **strengths** – of the Thessalonian church? They had faith, hope, and love. Their faith was so strong, in fact, that it was proclaimed all over the place. No **weaknesses** are identified in the two letters, but Paul emphasizes their faith and their love repeatedly, but then corrects them a little bit on their hope at the end. He doesn't say it's a weakness, but he adds a challenge regarding their hope. If I'm doing this SWOT, I would say for the Thessalonians it's a weakness. They needed some help with hope. What **opportunities** or external advantages did they have? With their location in Asia Minor they had access to communities. They had tremendous opportunity for message dissemination. What **threats** or external disadvantages did they have? They were encountering a lot of persecution, and it made things difficult. It actually impacted their hope, and it maybe exacerbated a potential weakness.

Let's look at the Corinthians. What are their strengths? They were in Christ, and that is the greatest strength of all. But what about their behavior? The Corinthians were horrible. They were an awful portrayal of what believers in Christ should be. Their list of strengths would be very short. One could add that they had tremendous equipping and training. So, perhaps two **strengths**. Their **weaknesses** would fill a very long list (or at least one long letter). They weren't applying their strengths. They weren't diligent. They were in disunity. They were arrogant. They were immoral. That is just for starters. They did have **opportunities** or external advantages. They had access to the finest teachers. They were in proximity to other churches and other believers who would come alongside and encourage them. They also encountered several **threats** and external disadvantages. They had persecution, and a host of idolatrous influences in the various religious systems represented at Corinth. These certainly made it more difficult for them to walk in Christ.

We can do a SWOT analysis on our own personal life or an organization, and it's a helpful tool for our gap analysis. Together, the SWOT and gap analysis help us recognize the gap between what we say we're doing and what we're actually doing. In fact, the SWOT analysis can slap us in the face with the reality of what especially those weaknesses are and what those threats are. Those expose how far we really are from actually doing what we say and think we are doing.

One final encouraging note about assessment. As Paul communicates with the Thessalonian believers, he doesn't rebuke them for any weakness. Rather he challenges them, saying, "I urge you to excel still more." Paul recognized that the Thessalonians were already doing the things he was prescribing – and everybody could see it. But the challenge still stands: excel still more. Get better. Continue to grow. Don't stop.

Regardless of where your organization is in this process in the cycle for excellence, and no matter whether it's a new organization or a more mature one, we always are faced with the task of being better and growing and advancing. It's a patently Biblical concept to excel still more. As you have the responsibility in leadership to guard yourself first as an individual, be certain you are doing the strategic planning and assessment in your own life personally. As leaders we also have similar responsibilities to those Paul communicated to Timothy: "Guard yourself and your teaching."[4] We have the responsibility as leaders in our organizations to ensure that the organization is exceling still more.

---

[4] 1 Timothy 4:16.

We are responsible to see that every member of our team has the tools and the investment (from us) they need in order to excel still more.